Prentice Hall
Foundations of Philosophy Series

Roderick M. Chisholm	Theories of Knowledge, 3/E
William Dray	Philosophy of History, 2/E
Joel Feinberg	Social Philosophy
William K. Frankena	Ethics, 2/E
Martin P. Golding	Philosophy of Law
Carl Hempel	Philosophy of Natural Science
John H. Hick	Philosophy of Religion, 4/E
Dale Jacquette	Philosophy of Mind
Stephen Nathanson	Economic Justice
Wesley C. Salmon	Logic, 3/E
Richard Taylor	Metaphysics, 4/E

Tom L. Beauchamp, Editor
Monroe Beardsley and Elizabeth Beardsley, Founding Editors

ECONOMIC JUSTICE

Stephen Nathanson

Northeastern University

PRENTICE HALL, Upper Saddle River, New Jersey 07458

Library of Congress Cataloging-in-Publication Data

NATHANSON, STEPHEN. [date]
Economic justice / Stephen Nathanson.
p. cm.
Includes bibliographical references and index.
ISBN 0-13-741844-2
1. Economics—Moral and ethical aspects. 2. Distributive justice.
3. Comparative economics. I. Title
HB72.N382 1998
330—dc21 97-5286

Editorial director: *Charlyce Jones Owen*
Acquisitions editor: *Angela Stone*
Production editor: *Edie Riker*
Cover photo: "Great Smokey Mountains National Park," W. Cody / Westlight
Buyer: *Tricia Kenny*
Marketing manager: *Jennifer Weinberg*
Editorial assistant: *Elizabeth Del Colliano*

This book was set in 10/12 Baskerville by East End Publishing Services and was printed and bound by Courier Companies, Inc. The cover was printed by Phoenix Color Corp.

Printed in the United States of America

10 9 8 7 6 5 4 3 2 1

ISBN 0-13-741844-2

Prentice-Hall International (UK) Limited, *London*
Prentice-Hall of Australia Pty. Limited, *Sydney*
Prentice-Hall Canada Inc., *Toronto*
Prentice-Hall Hispanoamericana, S.A., *Mexico*
Prentice-Hall of India Private Limited, *New Delhi*
Prentice-Hall of Japan, Inc., *Tokyo*
Simon & Schuster Asia Pte. Ltd., *Singapore*
Editora Prentice-Hall do Brasil, Ltda., *Rio de Janeiro*

Contents

Foundations of Philosophy

Many of the problems of philosophy are of such broad relevance to human concerns, and so complex in their ramifications, that they are, in one form or another, perennially present. Though in the course of time they yield in part to philosophical inquiry, they may need to be rethought by each age in the light of its broader scientific knowledge and deepened ethical and religious experience. Better solutions are found by more refined and rigorous methods. Thus, one who approaches the study of philosophy in the hope of understanding the best of what it affords will look for both fundamental issues and contemporary achievements.

Written by a group of distinquished philosophers, the *Foundations of Philosophy Series* aims to exhibit some of the main problems in the various fields of philosophy as they stand at the present stage of philosophical history.

While certain fields are likely to be represented in most introductory courses in philosophy, college classes differ widely in emphasis, in method of instruction, and in rate of progress. Every instructor needs freedom to change their course as their own philosophical interests, the size and make-up of his classes, and the needs of his students vary from year to year. The volumes in the Foundations of Philosophy Series—each complete in itself, but complementing the others—offer a new flexibility to the instructor, who can create his own textbook by combining several volumes as he wishes, and can choose different combinations at different times. Those volumes that are not used in an introductory course will be found valuable, along with other texts or collections of readings, for the more specialized upper-level courses.

Tom L. Beauchamp, Editor
Elizabeth Beardsley and Monroe Beardsley, Founding Editors

For Bea and Peter,
Loving parents-in-law,
Loyal fans

Preface

This book is about one of the most pressing and difficult problems of political philosophy and political life—the problem of economic justice. In writing the book, I have tried to achieve three aims. The first is to present the results of philosophical thinking about economic justice in a way that is clear and understandable. The second is to give my own answer to the question: What must a society do in order to be economically just? The third is to contribute to the creation of an economically just society.

These aims are related because one of the main obstacles to achieving a just society is that we lack a clear, socially shared understanding of the nature of economic justice. Widely different views are advocated, and there is both strife and confusion about what justice requires. I believe that philosophical reflection and analysis can help us arrive at a better understanding of the demands of justice.

In writing the book, I have combined my own best effort to construct a theory of economic justice with a discussion that can serve as an introduction to philosophical debates and theories in this field. I have tried to write a book that can be understood by people who are not already familiar with the many books and articles that scholars have written about economic justice. The discussion of these issues is too important to be limited to academic philosophers and other theorists. If the products of our best thinking are to have any influence in the world, some of us must strive to make theoretical work understandable to concerned citizens and students who are not scholars or professional thinkers.

The general issues I discuss will be familiar to anyone who reads the newspaper or watches television news. I approach these issues in a theoretical way, however, and do not generally relate them directly to the day's news. I do this for two reasons. First, questions about economic justice are not simply today's issues. They have been debated since biblical times and show every sign of remaining contentious for the foreseeable future. In addition, contemporary public debate is usually tied up with efforts to jockey for political power and influence. Often, people express ideas not to promote understanding but to gain office or discredit the opposition.

One of the virtues of a theoretical discussion is that it takes the issues themselves seriously and explores them in a more open-minded way. That is not to say that my discussion is neutral or that my inquiry is strictly scientific. Nonetheless, I try to describe and evaluate all the views I discuss in a fair and impartial way, and my discussion is guided and constrained by the aim of discovering the truth. If we can find the truth, then it can guide us in our personal and political activities, but during the inquiry, our thinking should not be determined by narrow interests or prereflective conclusions. We should be prepared to change our views as well as to defend them.

My strategy in the book is to focus on three different economic systems: capitalism, socialism, and the welfare state. Each of these systems presents a possible solution to the problem of economic justice. I describe each system, examine the reasons why some people favor it, and then consider criticisms that others raise against it. On the basis of these reflections, I defend a particular view about what a society must do in order to achieve economic justice.

In writing this book, I have benefited greatly both from the many thinkers whose works I have read and from the friends, colleagues, and students with whom I have discussed these problems. I am indebted to Northeastern University for the opportunity to teach courses dealing with this subject and to the students who have shared my inquiry into it. I have learned the most by being able to return to this subject many times in the courses I have taught. This has forced me to understand and explain the views of others and enabled me to test my own views against the reactions of students.

Special thanks are due to Steven Lee and John Post as well as to the Prentice Hall reviewers —Irfan A. Khawaja, University of Notre Dame, and Orville Clark, University of Wisconsin–Green Bay. Their reactions to the manuscript gave me both useful criticisms and much encouragement. Thanks, too, to Tom Beauchamp and Angela Stone for their interest in this project.

Finally, deepest thanks to my wife Linda and my children Michael and Sarah, my constant sources of inspiration and support.

CHAPTER ONE

Introduction

Questions about economic justice come up in many contexts. Like most important questions, they arise in daily life, and though they are discussed by philosophers and other scholars, they were not invented by them. In this chapter, I will describe some of the ways that questions about economic justice arise in daily life as well as some of the disagreements people have about these questions.

VAST DISPARITIES OF WEALTH

A familiar fact about the world is that the resources possessed by different people vary tremendously. To put the point bluntly but accurately, some people do not have enough resources to live a minimally decent life. They lack money, food, shelter, medical care, and other necessities of life. At the same time, other people live in great luxury, possessing more resources than they can possibly use and using some of these to purchase yachts, expensive jewelry, and other luxury items. Between these conditions of extreme wealth and extreme poverty, there are people at many different levels of economic well-being, some possessing much and others little. And, though a once popular song tells us that "the best things in life are free," the fact is that the amount of resources people possess plays a large (though not exclusive) role in determining how good a life they can lead.

The existence of these disparities gives rise to the problem of economic justice because the distribution of goods is not an unchangeable fact of nature; it is a social fact that is subject to human control. It could be changed if enough people thought it was wrong and wanted to change it. In fact, throughout history people have acted to change the distribution of resources, sometimes through charitable contributions, often through government programs, and occasionally through violent revolutions.

What should we think about these extreme disparities in people's possessions? Are they just or unjust? Should steps be taken to reduce or eliminate them?

Many people have thought that these disparities are unjust and that we should use the power of government to create a society in which such extremes of wealth and poverty would not exist. Other people have denied that this situation is unjust and have argued that it would be wrong for governments to interfere with the distribution of wealth and other goods.

ARE DISPARITIES DEFENSIBLE?

We may wonder how anyone could deny that such huge disparities in resources are a great injustice or that diminishing them to improve the lives of people in poverty is a moral imperative. Nonetheless, there are thoughtful people who deny these claims. Here are two arguments that are sometimes raised in defense of their reaction.

First, while virtually everyone agrees that poverty is bad for the people who endure it, some people deny that it is an injustice. After all, not everything bad that happens to people is an injustice, and so it is important to distinguish those bad things that are *misfortunes* from those that are *injustices*. While it is very bad for a child to be born with serious birth defects or for a person to be killed in an avalanche, there is nothing unjust about these situations. They are simply bad things that happen to people. No one is responsible for them. Similarly, it could be argued that while poverty is a misfortune, a bad thing that happens to people, it is not an injustice. No one is to blame for the uneven distribution of resources, and no one has an obligation to change it.

Second, even if governments could use tax money to prevent poverty, some thinkers argue that it is wrong to force people to assist those who are poor. Suppose, for example, that we decided to help the poor by adopting a Robin Hood strategy—robbing the possessions of the rich and giving them to the poor. Since robbery is wrong, this would be wrong to do, even if it had the effect of helping poor people. Why? Because it violates the rights of better-off people to control their money and other possessions. While Robin Hood has a perfect right to try to persuade well-off people to give their money to the poor, he has no right simply to take their money.

So, against the view that wide disparities are unjust and that there is a social duty to use government to alter the distribution of wealth, this objection says two things: first, that wide disparities of resources, even if they are bad for people who suffer from them, are not unjust; and, second, that forcing people to help the poor is itself an injustice, since it amounts to stealing people's possessions.

People who hold this view might acknowledge that it would be good if better-off people voluntarily provided help to the poor. They might even say that charity is a moral duty, but they deny that forced assistance through taxation or other governmental action is justified.

Beginning, then, with the same facts about wealth, poverty, and the wide disparities of possessions and well-being among people, different people come to very different moral conclusions. They differ over whether the disparities between rich and poor are an injustice or simply a misfortune, and they disagree over whether government programs to help the poor are morally right or wrong.

THE PROBLEM OF JUST WAGES

Questions of economic justice often come up when we think about the differences in pay associated with different occupations. One way to see this is to make a list of ten occupations and arrange them in order of what you would regard as an ideal pay scale. Who should make the most? Who the least? After making your list, see whether your ideal scale matches the way things are. If the actual pay scale varies from your ideal one, you may not think that the way things are is fair or just.

The view that current pay scales are unjust is forcefully expressed by Tom Cottle in an essay that compares the salaries of baseball players and teachers. He writes:

> Now that Robin Yount has signed a baseball contract for more than $3 million a year, he has something in common with my wife, a public school teacher. He will earn in 3 days what she earns in 9 and 1/2 months. Prior to Yount's signature, she already had this in common with Ricky Henderson and Mark Langston. Some would say this isn't fair, but at least she doesn't have to change clothes when she goes to work. . . . With Kirby Puckett, my wife shares two things: First, he will earn in one year twice what she will earn in 40 years. Second, they both stand less than 6 feet tall.[1]

It is hard not to sympathize with Cottle's bitter reaction to this situation. We live in a society that claims to value education, and most of us think that educating young people is an important task. Even lovers of baseball would admit that teaching children is at least as important as baseball. Moreover, with all due respect to baseball players, Mrs. Cottle probably works harder than Robin Yount or Ricky Henderson. The school season is longer than the baseball season, and in addition to the purely academic part of her work, she

[1] Tom Cottle, "Throwing a Curve at Our Teachers," *Boston Sunday Globe,* Focus Section, January 7, 1990.

WHAT'S AHEAD

In this introduction, I have described a few ways in which questions about economic justice arise in the course of our ordinary, nontheoretical activities. Questions about disparities of wealth, about salaries that seem too high or too low, and about both the demands and responsibilities of government often come up in ways that trouble and disturb us. These questions also divide us, since we disagree in our reactions to them. Disagreement can, of course, be healthy, but it can also sharpen divisions among people and make cooperation more difficult. For this reason, it is worth striving for a consensus about the nature of economic justice.

But how can we tell which views about economic justice are correct? How can we determine what counts as just in the distribution of economic resources?

Many people have tried to answer these questions. My attempt to describe the problems and to provide a solution will take the following form.

Chapter 2 describes three different kinds of economic systems: capitalism, socialism, and the welfare state. Each of these systems provides an answer to questions of economic justice and a model for how the economy should be governed.

Chapters 3 and 4 set the terms of the debate by describing both the main arguments given in favor of a pure form of capitalism (sometimes called "libertarian" capitalism), as well as the main arguments that socialists raise against capitalism and in defense of their own view.

Chapters 5, 6, and 7 contain evaluations of capitalism and socialism from the perspective of three questions: Which one better promotes human well-being? Which succeeds in giving people what they deserve? Which more effectively promotes people's liberty? In these chapters, I also explain the approach of welfare state advocates to these three questions, and I defend the view that a welfare state promotes these values (well-being, desert, and liberty) better than capitalism or socialism.

Chapter 8 describes and evaluates the influential views developed by John Rawls in *A Theory of Justice.* I explain Rawls's views and show how they lend support to a welfare state. I also argue that Rawls does not fully succeed in describing the requirements of economic justice.

In Chapter 9, I ask two questions about the welfare state: How extensive should such a state be? And, what resources should it guarantee to its citizens? I defend an extensive form of welfare state that I call the "comprehensive welfare state." In defending such a state, I describe the conditions a society must satisfy in order to meet the demands of economic justice and show how the comprehensive welfare state does this. Finally, Chapters 10 and 11 describe and respond to the most important objections against the comprehensive welfare state.

CHAPTER TWO

Three Views

The problems sketched in the introduction have generated many proposed solutions and many debates. Rather than investigating each issue separately, I am going to proceed by considering three overall systems of thought about economic justice and the distribution of resources. Each of these systems generates a different assessment of facts about wealth and poverty, and each gives rise to a different plan of action to deal with them.

The three views I will consider are those associated with capitalism, socialism, and the welfare state. This chapter contains brief descriptions of each view. In the rest of the book, I will consider the strongest arguments for and against each view and will seek to determine which one is best.

In order to prevent confusion, I should note at the start that my descriptions of these systems are not meant to portray any particular countries or societies. Virtually all actual societies incorporate inconsistent values and ideals; they are the result of historical compromises and happenstance. The systems I describe are ideals and thus have a clarity and consistency that existing economies lack. These ideals provide the standards by which their adherents judge actual societies.[1]

[1] For a similar distinction between ideals and actual systems, see Tibor Machan's preface to *The Main Debate: Communism vs. Capitalism* (New York: Random House, 1987), v–iv. He writes: "Capitalists, as understood here, do not regard the United States or Great Britain as fully capitalist systems, though they would agree that these countries come the closest to capitalism to date. . . . Nor need Marxian (socialist) theorists regard the Soviet Union or the People Republic of China as examples of the fully emancipated . . . socialist human communities."

CAPITALISM

Capitalism, like the other views I will consider, is both a theory and an economic system. It is a way of organizing an economy and a body of beliefs about how an economy ought to be organized. Since economic systems are quite complex, views about them must be complex as well. Matters are further complicated by the fact that there are different forms of capitalism.

In order to make these complexities manageable, I am going to do two things. First, my description of capitalism will focus on a relatively pure form that is sometimes called "libertarian capitalism." In many ways, it best captures the key features of the capitalist ideal, and it makes clear the contrasts between capitalism, socialism, and the welfare state.

Second, I am going to focus on three features of economic systems that are especially important from the point of view of economic justice. These are

1. a conception of property rights
2. a view about how goods should be produced and distributed
3. an allocation criterion for determining what share of resources should go to different people

By focusing on a small number of essential features, we will be better able to understand and compare the strengths and weaknesses of these systems.

With these three features in mind, I would describe capitalism as an economic system that is characterized by

1. private ownership of property
2. a market system of production and distribution
3. an allocation criterion that grants resources to people in accord with their market value, supplemented by gifts

Let me explain how I understand each of these.

PRIVATE OWNERSHIP OF PROPERTY

In a capitalist economy, resources are the property of individuals or groups of individuals, and the owners of property have the right to determine what should be done with it. This right has implications for other people as well, since having the right to determine what should happen to one's own property prevents other people from deciding what should be done with it.

To take a simple example, if I own a watch (as I do), then I have many rights with respect to this watch. I may take the watch with me when I go out or leave it at home. I may sell the watch to someone else, let someone borrow it for a while, or simply give it away as a gift. If I am angry or in a destructive mood, I may smash the watch. Because it is mine, I may do with it as I like.

These rights of ownership give me special powers concerning the watch that others don't have. Other people have no right to smash my watch, to take it without my permission, or sell it to a third party. All of those acts would violate my property rights, and in a system of law that recognizes and protects property rights, all of those acts are crimes.

In a purely capitalistic system, all property would be privately owned. Every item would be like my watch. There would be some person or group with wide powers to determine what should be done with it. For the most part, other people would have no right to interfere with the owner's decisions.

This is not to say that owners have absolute or unlimited rights to decide what to do with their property. For example, if I own a knife, my property rights do not permit me to place it point first in your body. That would be a violent offense against you. So property rights are limited or constrained by other rights that people have, such as the right to life or the right to be free from harmful assault. Nonetheless, in a system of private ownership, decisions about what to do with individual items like watches, knives, homes, or money are mostly left to the owners of those items.

Moreover, just as decisions about individual items are left to individuals who have property rights in them, the same is true of large-scale items of property, like land, buildings, or productive machinery. No distinction is made between items of personal property and the productive components of the economy.

While all of this may seem quite familiar and ordinary, it is worth noting that the ideal of a world of purely private property has quite radical implications. If all property were privately owned, there could be no government. In order for government to exist and carry out its functions, it needs to possess some property. Even if a government carries out only minimal tasks, such as providing police protection or punishing criminals, it needs some resources. It needs money to pay the police, and it needs to own uniforms and equipment so they can do their job. It needs the resources required to conduct trials (such as court rooms, record keeping equipment, and file cabinets). So, inevitably, where there is government, some property is publicly owned. This could not occur in a world of purely private ownership.

Similarly, because governments need resources to carry out their functions, they must collect taxes. That is, they must have the ability to take some property from individuals to use for public functions. Since individuals do not always want to contribute voluntarily, governments must be authorized to use coercive power to force citizens to pay taxes. In taking note of this, I do not mean either to approve or disapprove of this practice. (This is an issue for later discussion.) I simply want to point out that by having a government, we automatically limit the scope of both private property and private property rights. Some things will exist that are publicly rather than privately owned. And, people's rights to control privately owned resources will be limited by the government's rights to collect taxes. Any system of taxation presupposes that owners do not have the sole right to determine what to do with "their" money.

While a capitalist system, then, is characterized by private ownership, the extent to which things are privately owned may vary. In a capitalist society that was anarchistic and had no government, all property would be privately owned. In societies that have governments, some amount of resources (greater or lesser) will be publicly owned, and taxation will limit (to some degree) people's rights to use their property as they desire.

THE MARKET SYSTEM OF PRODUCTION AND DISTRIBUTION

Economic systems are systems of production and distribution. Human beings need various things in order to live, and very few people are able to produce everything they need for themselves or acquire them from nature. Things could be different. We can imagine a world in which everything we need literally grows on trees. In such an Eden-like world, people could simply go to the appropriate tree and pick what they want. This, however, is not our world.

Many things that we need or want must be produced by other people, so decisions have to be made about what goods to produce and how to distribute them. In a capitalist system, such decisions are left to individuals and to the workings of the market. People produce things or offer services that they think other people will want to buy. It is in the interests of individuals to offer things for sale that others want or need, so they have an incentive to produce things of value. Likewise, as consumers, individuals will seek out people selling goods they want or need. Thus, at least in theory, the things people need and want will be produced by someone, even though there is no overall system that deliberately coordinates the production of goods.

One advantage of such a system is that it is very flexible. Since it is hard to know all the things a society needs, the creation of a coordinated system of production would be quite difficult. While no individual or group could possibly know all the needs of a society, individual people can easily become aware that a particular need is not being met. For example, one person might see that residents of a particular town have to travel many miles to buy pizza, and she could infer that if she were to open a local pizza parlor, she would be able to sell pizza to them. The same type of thought process could be followed by many individuals, and in this way, the availability of desired goods could increase, even though there is no overall planning about what to produce.

A second function the market achieves is the determination of the price of goods. In a market system, price is a function of supply and demand. Where a product is scarce and many people want it, sellers can charge a lot. If one customer is not willing to pay the high price, others will do so. By contrast, if a product is plentiful, consumers can pay less because the seller has to worry about being left with many unsold goods. That is why farmers may make less money in "good" years when crops grow well: The more crops there are, the lower the price they will bring in.

Competition increases these pressures. Where more than one seller of a product exists, each seller has to provide an incentive for the buyer to take his product rather than to buy from the competition. One way to do this is to lower the price. Another is to increase the quality of product. The pizza maker can try to get people to buy pizza from her rather than the competition either by charging less or by making a better pizza (or both!). In this way, market pressures help consumers by giving producers and sellers an incentive to provide goods that are cheaper to buy and that have higher quality.

In short, the market system is supposed to provide the products people need at the lowest possible price and at the highest level of quality (for the price). And, it does this by an "invisible hand" rather than a central planning process.[2]

TO EACH, ACCORDING TO . . .

The third aspect of an economic system is its allocation criterion—its standard for determining what share of resources individuals are supposed to receive. Now, if we mean by resources the products sold in the market, then in a capitalist system the people who get resources are the ones who have money to pay for them. But how do people get money and what determines how much they get? Again, in a capitalist system, this is determined in large part by the market.

In the simplest case, people who sell products get whatever profit they can make from selling them. If they are successful, it may be a great deal of money; if they are unsuccessful, it may be very little.

What about a case where one person has a job working for another person? What determines that person's salary level? Here, the market mechanism of supply and demand is again relevant. If someone has a rare skill that is in high demand, that person will be able to obtain a high salary, since if one employer does not pay the desired rate, another will be willing to do so. If, however, a person has skills that are plentiful or for which there is little demand, he will not be able to get anyone to pay him a lot. Just as the market value of other goods and products is determined by the relationship between supply and demand, so the price of people's labor is determined in the same way. Within the market, then, the criterion for allocation of money to people is "to each, according to their market value."

The money or other goods that people have does not always come from working or from buying and selling. Sometimes, people receive things as gifts from others. When this happens, the new owner's right to the property arises because the original owner had a right to give it away. A libertarian capitalist system permits this kind of transfer. Because property rights can come into existence through gift giving, the allocation criterion for capital-

[2] Adam Smith, *The Wealth of Nations,* 5th ed., abridged (New York: The Modern Library, 1985), 225.

ism needs to be amended to read "to each, according to their market value plus gifts."

This addition may seem trivial if we think about the small presents people usually receive for birthdays or holidays. Gifts, however, can play a very significant function in a capitalist distribution system. For example, if people do not succeed in the market and cannot acquire enough resources to meet their needs, they may receive charitable gifts. Charity can serve as a buffer that gives some people protection from failure in the market. In a pure capitalist system, the buffer provided by charitable gifts can mean the difference between life and death.

Inheritances are a second, very important kind of gift, since they allow some people to acquire substantial resources without any work at all. If a parent wants to leave a large amount of money to a child or a benefactor to some favored person, the right to give gifts enables them to do so. In this way, success in the market can be passed on to successive generations in the same family or to others who are favored by the donor. Since much of people's total possessions consists of accumulated wealth rather than earnings from work, bequests and inheritances are an important feature of a libertarian capitalist economy.

SOCIALISM

Like capitalism, socialism comes in many different forms. I am going to focus on the version that is most important historically and that contrasts most sharply with libertarian capitalism. This is the system of "state socialism." Like libertarian capitalism, it has a distinctive conception of property rights, mechanisms of production and distribution, and a criterion of proper allocation. Socialism is characterized by

1. public ownership of property
2. a planned economy, with a centralized, publicly controlled system of production and distribution
3. an allocation criterion that grants resources to people in accord with their need

Let us look briefly at each of these features.

PUBLIC OWNERSHIP OF PROPERTY

In a socialist system, society as a whole is the primary owner of property. In a pure socialist system, there would be no private property at all. Just as we saw, however, that a capitalist system is bound to contain some public property, so too, a socialist system is likely to contain some private property.

Many of our everyday activities are made easier by our being assured access to particular things. Given that I need my watch every day, it would be very inconvenient if I did not have a primary claim on it. Likewise, it would be annoying and inconvenient if individuals did not have primary claims on items like toothbrushes or clothing. So some form of individual property rights is almost inevitable in a socialist society. Resources are unlikely to be always up for grabs, for that would lead not only to inconvenience but also to conflict and resentment.

For these sorts of reasons, it is usually understood that ordinary goods would be privately owned in a socialist society but that the "means of production" (the factories, materials, and equipment used to produce goods) would be publicly owned. This would be a distinctively socialist system, even though individuals would still own items for personal use.

A PLANNED ECONOMY

Socialists think that decisions about what goods should be produced are too important to be left to the unguided process of the market. Whereas capitalists are committed to a certain process (the workings of the market), socialists are committed to the achievement of certain results, and they believe that the economy should be organized with the specific aim of achieving those results.

What is it that socialists want to achieve? In a socialist society, the highest priority is given to meeting people's needs. Therefore, in a socialist society, the government would be responsible for surveying people's needs and desires, and it would allocate resources to produce those goods that are required to meet people's most important needs. Since all production uses resources, government planners would try to make sure that valuable resources are not squandered or used for goods of trivial value.

While state socialism is associated historically with the authoritarian politics of the Soviet Union, it is compatible with a variety of forms of economic decision making. The authority to make these decisions could be held by expert planners, by political leaders, or by citizens acting through democratic processes. Each of these procedures would give rise to a different form of state socialism. What is common to all of them is that decisions about production and distribution would be made with the goal of satisfying public needs, and they would be made by public officials or procedures rather than by private individuals.

A socialist economy might contain some elements of competition. For example, if too many people want a particular job, hiring might be done through a competitive application procedure. This procedure, however, would simply be a means for identifying the person best able to do the job, and the competition need not affect other things, like the salary paid for the work, for example. Hence, the role of competition would be much less significant than it is in a market economy. Instead, ideals of social cooperation and the desire to contribute to the good of society would be important sources of motivation.[3]

Finally, since the main priority in a socialist economy is meeting people's needs, there would have to be some procedure for distributing products to

[3] For examples of ways in which competition might continue to function in a socialist society, see Edward Bellamy's utopian socialist novel, *Looking Backward,* (New York: New America Library, 1960).

the right people. Once people's needs were established, they would have access to the goods suited to them.

TO EACH, ACCORDING TO . . .

Socialists believe that the primary criterion for allocation is need. They criticize capitalism for making people's ability to meet their needs depend on success in the marketplace. For socialists, the fact that people are hungry provides sufficient reason for them to receive food, and a person's illness would justify access to medical care. This is in contrast to a capitalist system, in which access to goods is determined not by people's needs but rather by their ability to pay.

Socialist economies could work in a variety of ways. In some, people could simply claim particular goods. In others, they might receive an amount of money sufficient for purchasing the things they need. While there might be some variation in people's earnings, the differences would usually be small, for socialism is motivated in part by an egalitarian vision. Since people are equal in value and importance, the large differences between rich and poor would not be permitted to arise. A socialist society would not be divided into economic classes.

For these reasons, individuals could not accumulate large amounts of wealth, and thus, even though gift giving would remain as a practice, there would be neither charity nor large monetary inheritances. Charity would be unnecessary because there would be no poor people who require charitable assistance to meet their needs. Large inheritances would not exist because the accumulation of wealth would be limited and because they would violate the egalitarian ideals that underlie the socialist view. Affection and concern for others would have to be expressed in ways that do not create or perpetuate economic inequalities.

THE WELFARE STATE

The third kind of system is the welfare state. It combines aspects of both capitalism and socialism. For this reason, some people see the welfare state as an uneasy compromise between two incompatible ideals, while others think it is a perfect compromise, combining the best of both views without the defects of either. While the welfare state is, in a sense, a hybrid system, I will treat it as a distinctive system in its own right, a system with its own set of values and ideals.

There are different possible types of welfare state. The type I will consider is often called "welfare capitalism." It is characterized by the following features:

1. primarily private ownership of property
2. a market system of production and distribution, supplemented by some government distribution of resources

3. an allocation criterion that grants resources to people in accord with their market value, supplemented by gifts and by guaranteed, publicly funded access to some economic resources

I will briefly describe each of these.

OWNERSHIP OF PROPERTY

In a system of welfare capitalism, most property, including the means of production, would be privately owned. In this respect, welfare statism is like capitalism. Nonetheless, because welfare statists think that the government has a necessary role in the working of the economy, they do not see state ownership as inherently undesirable. Unlike advocates of pure capitalism, welfare state advocates are not likely to be disturbed by the growth of government services or the large size of government bureaucracies. For them, big government is not necessarily bad government. If government services and bureaucracies achieve good results, they will be supported. If they have negative effects, then they will be resisted by welfare statists. The right size of government should be determined pragmatically, not by appeal to rigid principles.

Unlike socialists, welfare statists need not object to private property, and they may not oppose large accumulations of property by individuals. To the extent that the private property system works well, they would leave it intact. Welfare statists, then, begin with an acceptance of both public and private property and without a desire to see one or another form of property limited or diminished for its own sake.

If we consider the *amount* of property that is held privately or publicly, we can see that the types of welfare state form a continuum that stretches between the limits of ideal market capitalism and state socialism. On the one hand, a rather minimal welfare state would own little property and would approximate the libertarian capitalist end of the spectrum. On the other hand, a very extensive welfare state would own much property and could approach the state socialist end of the spectrum. So the mix of private and public ownership can vary among different welfare states. This mix may also vary within a particular state at different times. In wartime, for example, governments greatly increase the level of public holdings by purchasing weapons and constructing housing and other facilities for people in the military. In times of peace, these holdings might diminish. There is no single answer to the question of exactly what mix of public and private property must characterize a welfare state.

A MARKET DISTRIBUTION WITH SUPPLEMENTS

Advocates of welfare capitalism agree with libertarian capitalists that the market system has many valuable features, and they generally favor using the market as the primary means by which goods are produced and distributed. Likewise, they generally accept the fact that people's earnings will be largely determined by the market and that this will lead to disparities in income and well-being.

What is distinctive of welfare statists is that they do not believe that the market is entirely adequate. They believe that the state should use its power to alter the outcome that results from competition in the market. In their view, governments should allocate some resources to people independently of whether those people can succeed in the market. For example, if some people are unemployed or ill, states should provide them with the resources required to meet their needs. Welfare state theorists are not content, as libertarian capitalists are, to leave the meeting of these needs to the market and charity. In this sense, they accept the socialist's claim that we must attend to the *results* of an economic system, not just the *process* by which goods are produced and distributed. Likewise, they agree with socialists that meeting people's needs is a high priority.

So, while a pure market system distributes all goods in market exchanges or by voluntary gift giving, the welfare state allocates some goods to people outside of the market. It provides some things to people for free or at a subsidized rate, and it pays for these goods with money collected in taxes.

Just as welfare states vary among themselves in terms of the amount of property held by the government, so they also vary in terms of how extensive a range of goods they provide to people. A very minimal welfare state might provide only free food to the starving. A more extensive welfare state will provide free public education to all or guarantee housing or medical care to everyone. There is a broad spectrum of possibilities. The less extensive the goods and services provided, the more the welfare state will resemble a libertarian capitalist state. If extensive goods and services are provided, the welfare state will more closely resemble a socialist state.

In fact, while I have used the expression "welfare capitalism" to describe the welfare state, one could imagine such a state evolving out of a socialist system as well. This would happen if a state socialist regime began to turn over more and more productive property to private owners and allowed markets a greater role in determining prices and resource use. In recent years, some people have advocated "market socialism" as a way of meeting some of socialism's goals while using markets to supplement or replace central planning as a system of production.[4] Such systems would count as forms of the welfare state because they would guarantee citizens some access to resources and would incorporate a mix of publicly and privately owned property.

Different welfare state systems, then, form a continuum between the extremes of pure capitalism and pure socialism. There are many different possible systems because each system is characterized by several features and each feature allows for variation. Thus, there can be different ratios of private versus public property, stronger and weaker versions of individual property rights, more or less production and distribution left to the market,

[4] For a philosophical defense of market socialism, see David Miller, *Market, State, and Community* (Oxford: Oxford University Press, 1989).

more or less resources that are guaranteed to citizens, and so on. Welfare systems, then, can take many different forms. In all of them, however, some degree of distribution by the market is supplemented by some degree of government-funded, legally guaranteed distribution of resources to citizens.

TO EACH, ACCORDING TO . . .

The allocation criterion for a welfare state, then, is that resources should be distributed to people in accord with their market value, supplemented by gifts and by guaranteed, publicly funded access to some share of economic resources.

In welfare states, the market continues to operate as a competitive system, and the results of that competition are recognized as legitimate. If people do well in the market, they will possess more than people who do poorly. In this way, welfare capitalism differs from state socialism, since it permits inequalities. In addition, like libertarian capitalism, welfare states permit gifts and thus leave room both for charity and for inheritances.

Nonetheless, like socialism, welfare statism recognizes claims on resources that do not grow out of market success or connection to generous donors. Within a welfare state, citizens are granted legal rights to some range of resources simply on the basis of their needs and the contribution that these resources can make to their well-being. The welfare state, like socialism, is organized around the idea that the economy is a public institution with a purpose. That purpose is to provide at least some minimal level of well-being to all citizens.

Of course, people who agree about the desirability of such a system may disagree strongly about the level of well-being that the state should guarantee to all citizens. Some people favor a minimum of relief from dire deprivation, while others favor a generous provision of goods, a level of resources that enables people not merely to survive but also to have a good chance for a happy, meaningful life. Given this range of differences, it is clear that people who agree about the desirability of a welfare state may differ among themselves as strongly as they do with the advocates of pure capitalism and pure socialism.

SUMMING UP

In this chapter, I have described the three main contenders for people's philosophical allegiance on the subject of economic justice. I have focused on economic systems rather than on philosophical theories of justice because our most basic choices involve the selection of systems and institutions. As we shall see, particular theories and even particular arguments can be appealed to by advocates of different systems. Likewise, different theories may converge in giving support to one system. So, our primary focus needs to be on the choice of a system. The value of philosophical theories depends on the extent to which they help us to make this choice.

CHAPTER THREE

The Case for Libertarian Capitalism

There are many arguments for a libertarian capitalist system. They can be found in the writings of philosophers, economists, and other theorists as well as in the popular culture of some societies. In this chapter, I will present what I see as the three most important arguments for capitalism. Not every advocate of market capitalism would be equally happy with all of them. Nonetheless, they do fit together in a rough way, and their apparent coherence strengthens their overall force.

Before setting out these arguments, I should emphasize that they are arguments for a pure, libertarian form of capitalism. As I noted earlier, the word "capitalism" is used loosely to describe many kinds of systems, including welfare state systems. The system I want to focus on has the following three features:

1. private ownership of property
2. a market system of production and distribution
3. an allocation criterion that distributes resources to people in accord with their market value, supplemented by gifts

The arguments I will consider claim that a system with these features is the best economic system because

1. It is the most productive and therefore creates the highest levels of well-being.
2. It is the most just because it rewards people in accord with how hard they work and how much they contribute to the good of society.
3. It respects people's personal liberty and helps to prevent political oppression.

Some defenders of capitalism may appeal to only one of these arguments, claiming it to be sufficient, but if all of them are valid, that would indeed present a forceful case for a capitalist system. If capitalism maximizes people's level of well-being, provides just rewards for work, and respects individual liberty, it is hard to see why anyone would reject it.

PRODUCTIVITY AND WELL-BEING

The appeal to capitalism's high productivity and its positive impact on human well-being is extremely important, even though it is not directly an appeal to justice. It is important because economic systems must actually work in practice. They must succeed in producing and distributing goods for people's use. If an ideal economic system satisfies our highest moral standards but fails to be workable and productive, then it would be rejected out of hand. Economic systems have to work.

The claim that capitalism makes people best off is actually a double argument. As a practical argument, it says that capitalism does best what economic systems are supposed to do—it produces goods and services. As a moral argument, it says that because capitalism produces the best results for all those who are affected, by it, it would be morally right (or just) to choose capitalism over its competitors.

In evaluating this argument, we need to ask three questions: (a) Is it true that capitalism makes people better off than any other system?; (b) if it does, what is the moral relevance of this fact?; and (c) if it does maximize well-being, is that sufficient to show that it is a just system?

Many people think it is obvious that capitalism is the best system for producing human well-being. The most wealthy and prosperous nations call themselves "capitalist" societies, while societies such as the former Soviet Union, which attempted to organize socialistically, have given up this effort and are trying to create market capitalist institutions. What more evidence could one want?

While these facts are powerful evidence, there are some important qualifications to them. First, none of the societies that we think of as "capitalist" exemplify a pure, libertarian form of market economy. All of them are welfare states of one sort or another. For this reason, we need to determine how much of their success results from the workings of the market and how much is a result of government intervention in economic matters.

Second, even if current capitalist systems are better producers of well-being than other existing systems, we might be able to create novel systems that produce even higher levels of well-being. If we can, then they will be superior to capitalism.

This last point is not meant to suggest that we compare capitalism with impossible utopian schemes. Nor is it meant to detract from its successes. Rather, the point is that capitalism might be capable of improvement or replacement. A full consideration of its value must compare it not only with existing alternatives but also with feasible, possible alternatives.

With these qualifications in mind, it is still possible for defenders of capitalism to cite the historic successes of its closest approximations as evidence for the productiveness of its ideal form. Peter Berger, on the basis of his examination of the historical evidence, draws the following conclusions about (largely) capitalist systems:

> Industrial capitalism has generated the greatest productive power in human history.
>
> To date, no other socioeconomic system has been able to generate comparable productive power. . . .
>
> An economy oriented toward production for market exchange provides the optimal conditions for long-lasting and ever-expanding productive capacity based on modern technology.[1]

Berger acknowledges that capitalism's high productivity might not be distributed in ways that benefit everyone, and he concedes that the early stages of industrial capitalism were marked by high human costs. Nonetheless, he concludes,

> Advanced industrial capitalism has generated, and continues to generate, the highest material standard of living for large masses of people in human history.[2]

Though Berger's claims are based on a survey of historical research, they are not much different from what many people claim to know as a matter of common sense, and they provide a powerful basis of support for capitalism.

There is something both intriguing and paradoxical about this argument for capitalism, however, for it claims that the best way to aim at the result of maximizing human well-being is by not striving directly to bring it about. Market capitalism maximizes productivity, even though no one in such a system strives for that result. Each producer and consumer, buyer and seller, employer and worker has his or her own private reasons for participating in the market, and yet, as Adam Smith suggested with his metaphor of the "invisible hand," the result of this process of self-seeking is the highest level of public well-being possible.

This is not to say that no one suffers in a capitalist economy. As a competitive system, a capitalist economy necessarily contains losers as well as winners. Nonetheless, the argument claims, the overall result is better than could be expected from any other economic system. As F.A. Hayek, one of market capitalism's most distinguished defenders, argues, the effects of a system of free market transactions, "though they always will harm some, are likely to improve the chances of all." A free market, he says, is the only sys-

[1] Peter Berger, *The Capitalist Revolution* (New York: Basic Books, 1986), 36–37.

[2] Ibid., 43

tem in which it is in "the interest of all so to conduct themselves as to make as large as possible the aggregate product."[3]

THE UTILITARIAN ARGUMENT

According to utilitarianism, if these claims about libertarian capitalism are true, then they would show that this system is the best one, both practically and morally. For utilitarians, the overall level of well-being produced by actions or policies is the sole standard by which we determine their rightness or wrongness. As Jeremy Bentham, one of the most influential advocates of the "principle of utility," explained,

> An action . . . [is] conformable to the principle of utility . . . when the tendency it has to augment the happiness of the community is greater than any tendency to diminish it. . . . Of an action that is conformable to the principle of utility one may always say either that it is one that ought to be done, or at least that it is not one that ought not to be done.4

Bentham's idea is that whenever we act, we should consider the possible actions before us and select the one that will produce more well-being than any other possible action. We should aim, as he said, for "the greatest happiness of the greatest number." When advocates of capitalism recommend it by virtue of its good overall effects on human well-being, they are appealing to this utilitarian standard.

In spite of its plausibility, there are two concerns about the utilitarian criterion that are relevant here. First, advocates of market capitalism should see that whatever support capitalism receives from the utilitarian standard is conditional. Utilitarians are not ideologically committed to capitalism. They are only committed to it as long as it is more successful at producing human well-being than other systems. If other systems, either actual or possible, are better at improving human well-being, then utilitarians will support those other systems. So, there is no intrinsic connection between utilitarianism and capitalism.[5]

Second, while utilitarians present their principle as the sole standard by which to judge actions and policies, there is reason to doubt this claim. As many critics of utilitarianism have argued, it is possible to imagine actions or policies that are immoral even though they maximize overall well-being.

Suppose, for example, that we could maximize the overall productivity of our economy by enslaving a small part of the population. While slavery

[3] F.A. Hayek, *The Mirage of Social Justice*, Volume 2 of *Law, Legislation and Liberty* (London: Routledge and Kegan Paul, 1976), 122.

[4] Bentham, *Introduction to the Principles of Morals and Legislation,* Book I, chapter iv, section x. Reprinted in *The Utilitarians* (Garden City, N.Y.: Dophin Books, 1961).

[5] John Stuart Mill, for example, was quite sympathetic to socialist criticisms of capitalism, even though he remained wary of the prospects for socialism's success. For his discussion, see his *On Socialism* (Buffalo, N.Y.: Prometheus Books, 1987; original ed., 1879).

would be bad for those who suffered from it, if the gains in well-being for the rest of the population were sufficiently large, this could outweigh the losses incurred through enslavement. *If* this were to occur, then utilitarians would be committed to supporting such a slave system, even though its arrangements appear to constitute a grave injustice.[6]

While I cannot fully discuss the merits and demerits of utilitarian morality here, I raise this criticism to suggest that a system might be morally unsatisfactory even if it promotes overall well-being better than its competitors. If slavery is unjust and therefore morally unacceptable (even if it would maximize overall well-being), it follows that utilitarian success is not sufficient to show an economic system to be morally acceptable. In addition, such systems must satisfy the criteria of justice.

There are two reasons, then, why defenders of market capitalism might not want to rely entirely on appeals to utility. First, these appeals may not always work in their favor. Libertarian capitalists may want a defense of their view that is less contingent on facts and more firmly based on principle than the utilitarian argument. Second, as the example of slavery suggests, even if facts about productivity support capitalism, they may not prove its moral worthiness. For this reason, defenders of capitalism often try to show that capitalism is superior not merely from the perspective of maximizing productivity but also from the perspective of justice. One way to do this is by arguing that capitalism is just because it is gives people what they deserve.

REWARDS FOR THE DESERVING

One of our most basic ideals of justice is that people ought to be treated in ways they deserve. According to this view, in an ideally just world, good people would enjoy benefits while bad people would suffer. In practice, of course, the evaluation of people is a difficult matter, and the idea of authorizing public agencies to determine people's degree of moral worth raises legitimate fears about abuse of government power.

Nonetheless, the idea of desert is a powerful one, and it plays an important role in our thinking about two areas of social life—the punishment of criminals and the establishment of economic rewards. Theorists often talk of just punishments and just rewards as two different departments of thought, calling the first "retributive" justice and the second "distributive" justice, but it is possible to see both ideas as aspects of one overall conception.

Suppose, for example, that we think that what someone deserves depends on the value of their contribution to society. From this perspective, the just way to treat people who make a positive contribution is to reward them, while the just way to treat those who make a negative contribution is to punish them. Someone who provides valuable economic goods and services

[6] For an interesting discussion of slavery from a utilitarian point of view, see R. M. Hare, "What is Wrong with Slavery?" *Philosophy and Public Affairs* 8 (1979); reprinted in Peter Singer, ed., *Applied Ethics* (New York: Oxford University Press, 1979).

should be rewarded for positive contributions, while someone who commits crimes and thus has a negative impact on others should be punished. Moreover, the amount of the reward or punishment should be proportional to the magnitude of the person's positive or negative contributions. People who benefit others more should get bigger rewards, while those who commit more serious crimes and thus do more harm to others should receive more severe punishments.

According to this view, justice requires a kind of reciprocity. In an ideal society, what people would receive for themselves would mirror what they have given to others.

In certain aspects of economic life, a market economy appears to conform to this ideal. As we saw earlier, the cost of an object or service (and thus the price that a seller can receive for it) depends in part on the demand for it. And, one would think, the demand for it would depend on the value that people attribute to it. The more valuable it is to them, the stronger is their desire for it, and the greater is their willingness to pay for it. This suggests that people's willingness to pay more for something depends on their assessment of its value and that people who offer goods of greater value will be able to sell them at higher prices. In this way, the amount received by people for the things they produce will vary with its value to others. The greater the contribution their product makes, the more likely that they will receive a higher price for it.

Our assessments of what people deserve do not always focus on what they actually produce. Sometimes we think that what people deserve depends on their efforts or how hard they work. Here, too, there are situations in which a market economy appears to offer rewards in proportion to what people deserve. Imagine that two people work for an hourly wage. One works forty hours per week, while the second wants to earn more and thus does additional hours of overtime work as well. In this situation, the person who works more will earn more, and this seems appropriate.

While these examples support the idea that capitalism rewards desert, it would be naive for defenders of capitalism to claim that people who work harder and make more valuable contributions always earn more than those who work less hard or do not contribute positively to others. Factors other than effort and contribution play important roles in determining levels of economic reward.

Nonetheless, many people appear to value capitalism for its tendency to reward superior efforts and superior contributions. If it does not always succeed in accomplishing these aims, that might simply show that there is room for improvement in the system. It does not show that other systems would do a better job at rewarding people in accord with what they deserve. In particular, since both socialists and welfare statists favor giving some resources to all people even if they make no positive efforts or contributions, both of those views appear to reject entirely the idea of rewarding people for their efforts and contributions. Capitalism, even if it fails to achieve the goal of rewards in accord with desert, at least appears to recognize it and to implement it to some degree.

LIBERTY AND JUSTICE: THE ENTITLEMENT THEORY

One of the most powerful arguments for capitalism links the libertarian concern for freedom with a conception of justice that emphasizes the moral right of property owners to do what they want with their own possessions. In *Anarchy, State, and Utopia,* Robert Nozick develops this freedom-based argument and deliberately avoids claims that capitalism maximizes well-being or gives people what they deserve. Nozick appeals to the simple but powerful idea that people are entitled to do what they want with their "holdings" (the things they legitimately own). He argues that as long as people engage in voluntary transfers of their holdings, the results of those transfers are just.

Justice, according to Nozick, is achieved through a process of voluntary exchanges. As long as the right procedure is followed in exchanges of holdings, the result is a just one. As Nozick puts it, "Whatever arises from a just situation by just steps is itself just."[7] Injustice occurs when exchanges are done improperly, as in cases of fraudulent or coercive transfers of property. When they are free and uncoerced, their results are just.

According to Nozick, a capitalist economy is just because it is simply the practice of people using their resources as they wish to. People freely create goods and services, and they engage in exchanges with other people, trading things they hold for things that others possess. Sometimes what people exchange is their own labor, consenting to work for others in exchange for money or other goods. Sometimes people simply give their holdings to others without getting anything in return. These transfers include personal gifts, acts of charity, and the passing on of inheritances. The economy as a whole is simply the sum total of the multitude of uncoordinated, individual actions. As long as these actions are free and voluntary, the resulting economic order is a just one.

For Nozick, libertarian capitalism is the only just economic system because it alone respects people's free choices and voluntary actions. It does not specify in advance that the distribution of holdings should conform to a particular pattern. Rather, it is a "historical" view that accepts whatever outcome arises from people's free choices. In a now famous example, Nozick describes a situation in which people willingly pay extra money (in addition to the regular price of admission) to see Wilt Chamberlain play basketball. Because many people are willing to pay extra money and because it goes directly to Chamberlain, he ends up with much more money than other people. Yet, Nozick claims, there can be nothing the matter with this because it is the result of many free decisions by individuals. If each person is entitled to pay extra money to see Chamberlain play and does so voluntarily, then there can be nothing unjust in Chamberlain's possessing all this money. The justice of this result follows from the justice of the process by which he acquired the money.

[7] Robert Nozick, *Anarchy, State, and Utopia* (New York: Basic Books, 1973), 151.

Generalizing from this example, Nozick claims that we cannot tell whether a distribution of resources is just simply by looking at how much is possessed by particular people. Instead, we must look at how people got what they possess. If they got it through legitimate means, then their possession is legitimate. How much they have in relation to other people is irrelevant.

THE CASE AGAINST GOVERNMENT INTERVENTION

If the result of free transactions is a just distribution, then, Nozick argues, any attempt to interfere with that distribution is immoral. It follows that the government's role must be limited to protecting the process of free exchanges. It is legitimate, for example, for government to prohibit robbery and fraudulent transactions, since these are coercive, illegitimate forms of transfer. The robbery victim does not choose to give her money to the thief, and the victim of fraud only gives up his money because he expects something in return that he will not receive. Likewise, if forced exchanges have occurred, government can transfer holdings to the original, rightful owners. This would achieve justice by rectifying a previous injustice.

As long as exchanges are voluntary, however, any government interference with them or with their results would be wrong. Suppose that laws were passed that forbid very large accumulations of wealth by individuals like Wilt Chamberlain. One way to implement such laws would be to prohibit people who want to pay extra to see Chamberlain play from doing so. More generally, the state would have to prevent people from engaging in any transfers that result in some individuals acquiring a great deal of wealth. This policy, Nozick says, would require "continuous interference in people's lives." It would require government to forbid "capitalist acts between consenting adults."[8]

Nozick's point is related to a political argument often made for capitalism. If we are concerned that large, powerful governments may become oppressive, we will look for ways to maintain large areas of individual freedom in people's lives. One way to do this is to reject policies that enable governments to engage in such interference. Nozick claims that if a society seeks to impose a pattern on how economic resources are distributed, it will be necessary for government to interfere with people's liberty in intrusive ways. It will be forced to prevent innocent activities such as paying more to see a particular basketball player. Nozick is certainly correct that such a policy appears intrusive and unattractive. If we value freedom, it will not appeal to us.

What if the government permits people to pay extra to see Chamberlain but then imposes heavy taxes on him so as to prevent him from amassing great wealth? This would not interfere directly with as many people. Nonetheless, it might result in everyone being less well off, since Chamberlain might not play under these conditions. This would deprive him of extra money and would deprive lovers of basketball from the opportunity to see him.

In addition, by requiring Chamberlain to pay heavy taxes, the government is engaging in a nonvoluntary, coercive transfer. The transfer of money

[8] Ibid., 163.

from Chamberlain to the tax collectors is coercive because failure to give the money is a criminal offense and could result in his being punished. The situation, from the libertarian perspective, is not morally different from a robbery. In both cases, one party uses the threat of force to coerce others to give away some of their money. This form of taxation, then, is an unjust transfer of holdings. It violates Chamberlain's right to do what he wants with the money he has received. Any law that authorizes the government to collect such taxes violates people's rights to do what they want with their own holdings. As such, it violates Nozick's procedural (free transfer) criterion of justice.

Nozick does not see his procedural criterion of justice as a merely legalistic or formal ideal. Rather, it is rooted in the deep moral value of giving proper respect to individuals. Nozick cites Kant's principle that one should always regard people as "ends in themselves" and never use them "as means alone."[9] We respect people by not using them as instruments for the good of others. Slavery's deepest offense is found in just this fact—that it uses some people solely as means for the well-being of others. According to Nozick, some forms of taxation have this same feature.

While many people think it is legitimate for governments to tax wealthy people in order to help the poor, Nozick rejects this idea. He believes that taxation for the purpose of providing such aid is "on a par with forced labor."[10] The person taxed is being used as a means for raising the well-being of others. There is no problem, of course, if someone voluntarily contributes to others. Taxation for this purpose, however, is a coercive and not a voluntary transfer of resources. Such forced transfers, he believes, violate our most basic moral principles regarding the proper treatment of other human beings.

For Nozick, then, the only legitimate role for government in the economy is to protect the process of voluntary exchange. If it goes beyond this and tries to determine the pattern of the resulting distribution, it is acting unjustly. The merit of a capitalist economy is that it respects people's rights and their freedom to engage in voluntary transactions. It does this by not trying to shape the resulting distribution of holdings in accord with some ideal pattern. Since both socialist economies and welfare states seek to enforce a particular distribution of goods, one that differs from what results from voluntary transfers, such systems are necessarily unjust. Libertarian capitalism is the only just system.

THE OVERALL ARGUMENT

The most powerful case for capitalism would join all three of these arguments. It would claim that capitalism makes people better off than any other economic system, that it more successfully rewards people in accord with what they deserve, and that it protects people's freedom to use their possessions as they wish.

[9] I. Kant, *Grounding for the Metaphysic of Morals,* James Ellington, trans. (Indianapolis, Ind.: Hackett Publishing, 1981), 36.

[10] Nozick, *Anarchy, State, and Utopia*, 169.

It is worth noting, however, that the criteria implicit in each of these arguments differ from one another and might give conflicting appraisals of capitalism. In particular, Nozick's entitlement theory focuses on the process by which goods are distributed rather than on the result of this process. In contrast, both the utilitarian argument and the desert argument are concerned with results or patterns of the sort Nozick rejects.

Utilitarians favor the system whose overall benefits are larger than the benefits of alternative systems, and they pay no special attention to the process by which these results are generated. That is why utilitarians run into a problem with slavery. Since they are indifferent to how things are produced and care only about the net balance of benefits over losses, they are in a weak position to condemn slavery when its benefits are sufficiently large. And, unlike Nozick, they are not specially wedded to a process of free exchange except insofar as this process maximizes well-being.

Likewise, people who want to provide just rewards for hard work or significant contributions are also concerned with the results of the distributive process. They have an ideal pattern in mind that they would like to see mirrored in the economy. They want people's holdings to be proportional to their degree of personal desert. Hence, like the utilitarians and unlike libertarians, they are concerned with outcomes and not merely with the processes by which holdings are distributed.

There is room, then, for conflict between proponents of these three arguments. Nonetheless, in their ideal world, defenders of capitalism would appeal to all three arguments, and if they could do so, they would have a very powerful case for a libertarian capitalist economy.

SUMMING UP

In this chapter, we've seen that defenders of capitalism can appeal to three strong arguments in favor of their system. Since we have not yet examined alternative systems, it would be premature to decide whether the advocates of capitalism have succeeded in showing it to be best.

Even at this stage, however, we can see that these arguments have a double value. In addition to showing why some people favor capitalism, these arguments also provide us with a set of criteria that we can use in evaluating any economic system. They help us focus on the basic questions we should ask about any system: How well off does it make people? Does it reward people in accord with what they deserve? And, what is its impact on people's liberty?[11]

[11] The three values picked out in these questions are the focus of discussion in Scott Gordon, *Welfare, Justice, and Freedom* (New York: Columbia University Press, 1980).

CHAPTER FOUR

Socialism and the Critique of Capitalism

Socialism, like capitalism, is both an ideology and a system. Socialists have their own distinctive view about how an economic order should be organized. As we have seen, the core of this view involves three basic features:

1. public ownership of property
2. a planned economy, with a centralized, publicly controlled system of production and distribution
3. an allocative criterion that distributes resources to people in accord with their need

As this list makes clear, socialism has its own positive program, and it can be described without even mentioning capitalism. Nonetheless, the two systems are joined historically because socialism arose as a reaction to the growth of capitalism. For this reason, some of the basic arguments *for* socialism take the form of arguments *against* capitalism. If socialists had not been radically dissatisfied with capitalism, they would not have worked to develop an alternative to it.

In considering the arguments for socialism, then, we can begin with socialist criticisms of the arguments for capitalism that we have just examined. Recall that the defense of capitalism consists of three main arguments:

1. Capitalism is the most productive system and therefore creates the highest levels of well-being.
2. Capitalism is the most just because it gives people what they deserve, rewarding hard work and high contributions to social good.
3. Capitalism respects people's personal liberty and helps to prevent political oppression.

The main case for socialism begins with an attack on each of these. According to socialists,

1. Capitalism fails to maximize human well-being.
2. Capitalism fails to give people their just deserts because it does not reward hard work or productivity.
3. Capitalism does not respect personal liberty.

In addition to these negative arguments, of course, socialists must also show that their system does a better job of meeting these or other proper criteria. If it accepts these criteria, it must show that

1. Socialism maximizes human well-being.
2. Socialism gives people what they deserve.
3. Socialism respects and enhances personal liberty.

The socialist argument, then, must include both a negative critique of capitalism and a positive argument that it can succeed where capitalism fails.

DOES CAPITALISM MAXIMIZE HUMAN WELL-BEING?

Defenders of capitalism often stress the fact that it is an enormously productive system. This fact is not denied by socialist critics. In the *Communist Manifesto,* for example, Karl Marx and Friedrich Engels stress the astounding productive growth that the capitalist class (or "bourgeoisie") has created. They write:

> The bourgeoisie, during its rule of scarce one hundred years, has created more massive and more colossal productive forces than have all preceding generations together. Subjection of Nature's forces to man, machinery, application of chemistry to industry and agriculture, steam-navigation, railways, electric telegraphs, clearing of whole continents for cultivation, canalisation of rivers, whole populations conjured out of the ground—what earlier century had even a presentiment that such productive forces slumbered in the lap of social labour?[1]

Marx, Engels, and other socialists do not deny that the development of capitalism created an enormous increase in the goods that people can produce.

The problem, however, is that an increase in the total amount of goods available does not automatically raise the overall level of human well-being. To see this, we need to distinguish between the *total* amount of goods produced and the way in which these goods are *distributed* among people. If most of these goods are owned and enjoyed by a relatively small group of people while the vast majority are denied access to them, then the growth in total productivity will not bring about a proportionate increase in human well-being. This is exactly what socialists claim occurs under capitalism. While a large share of the goods produced go to a relatively small group of

[1] Karl Marx and Friedrich Engels, *The Communist Manifesto* (New York: W.W. Norton, 1988), 59.

people, many people continue to live in poverty. Capitalism, while it succeeds in *producing* goods that could enhance human well-being, does not succeed in *distributing* goods in a way that actually has this effect. It maximizes production without maximizing well-being.

This criticism can be put in utilitarian terms, borrowing the concept of "marginal utility" from economics. Suppose that we want to distribute one hundred apples in the most beneficial way to one hundred people. We will not give them all to one person, leaving the other ninety-nine without anything. Why not? Because the value of each apple depends on how many other apples a person has. If the recipient of all the apples is hungry, then the first apple will have a certain positive value for her, and the second may as well. Even if she can still eat more, the third or fourth apple will have less value to her because she is no longer hungry. Apples five and six might actually make her sick, and if she cannot successfully store the rest for future use, they may go bad and thus contribute nothing to her well-being. It is because the additional apples have less value to this person that economists speak of their "declining marginal utility." Beyond a certain point of accumulation, all goods, including money, start to diminish in value.

In a society in which there are large disparities in wealth, one could do more good by redistributing some resources from the wealthy to the poor. Why? Because the wealthy already have enough both to satisfy their needs and to purchase many luxuries. More money for them will not appreciably raise their level of well-being. If money is directed toward those who are poor, however, it can be used in ways that will make a big difference to them—the difference between being fed and going hungry, for example, or being sheltered and being cold.

What these examples show is that we cannot get the maximum value out of goods if their possession is concentrated in a small part of the population. More good could be created by them if they were distributed more widely and more evenly.

THE DISTRIBUTION OF WEALTH

This utilitarian criticism of capitalism assumes, of course, that in a capitalist society, wealth will be distributed very unevenly, with some possessing much while others have very little. Notice, however, that this unequal distribution is a byproduct of capitalism and not a part of the capitalist's ideal.

Nonetheless, whether or not defenders of capitalism favor economic inequality, socialist critics see this unequal division of goods among rich and poor as a historically necessary outgrowth of capitalism. According to socialists, severe inequalities are an inevitable result of capitalism. They give different reasons for this, but two seem especially plausible in accounting for a tendency of the rich to get richer and the poor to become poorer.

The first reason is that gains and losses are cumulative. If a person begins with more resources than others or has some early successes, that person's gains can be invested to earn more money. In addition to earning some income by work, this person's investments can be earning extra gains at the same time. A person who does poorly and falls into debt has to struggle just to get back to his starting point. Working to pay off his debts, he will lack the funds either to buy things he needs or to invest anything for future return.

This process can continue over the long term. If a successful person passes on accumulated wealth to children or grandchildren, then these younger generations will be both more comfortable and better able to compete effectively in the market. They will probably be healthier, better educated, and in possession of money to invest in opportunities if they arise. At the same time, the children and grandchildren of unsuccessful people will start off with serious competitive disadvantages. They may be less healthy and may lack opportunities to develop useful skills to offer in the marketplace. Hence, the odds of their doing well are slim.

To bring out the force of this reasoning, imagine playing a succession of games of Monopoly™. In the first game, play proceeds as usual, with everyone starting out with $1500 from the bank. The second game, however, begins with every one holding the money they had at the end of the first game; the third begins with players holding the money they had at the end of the second, and so on. It does not take much insight to see that those who do well in the first game will have a distinct advantage as they enter the second, while those who do poorly will have a difficult time making a comeback. In the game, as in life, economic success tends to be cumulative. Those with more resources are in a better position to do well than are those with limited resources.

The second reason for these growing disparities between rich and poor has to do with the labor market. As we saw earlier, how much people are paid for work depends on the supply of and demand for labor. If there is a large pool of people in need of work, then employers need only offer low wages. What one worker will refuse as too little will be snatched up by others.

With this in mind, we can see why the rise of industrialism lowered workers' wages. It did this by both increasing the labor supply and decreasing the demand. As Marx and Engels argue, the invention of machines to perform many tasks reduces the demand for skilled craftsmen. They are no longer needed; instead, one only needs relatively unskilled workers to tend the machines in their work. This both lowers the demand for workers (since the machine does the equivalent of what many people had done), and it increases the supply by making almost anyone qualified for the work. Even children could be brought into factories, thus increasing the size of the labor pool and driving down wages to lower levels.

Some might argue that these developments were part of nineteenth-century capitalism but deny that the same pressures exist now. Nonetheless, these appear to be structural features of a capitalist system rather than transient aspects of capitalism during one era. A current issue of concern is the exporting of jobs to countries with lower wage scales, and this is simply an extension of the phenomenon I have described. By internationalizing the labor pool, the wages of higher-paid workers are undercut through the hiring of workers in poorer nations. In addition, the further development of technology continues to diminish the need for human labor in many areas of work, leading to the downsizing of many companies.

The tendency toward income disparities can also be seen in various economic statistics about income distribution in the United States. According to the Congressional Budget Office, between 1977–1988, annual income of families in the bottom 40 percent of the U.S. population declined, with those in the lowest decile declining by 10.5 percent. The largest gains in income were found in the upper 10 percent of the population, with gains in annual income averaging 27.4 percent. Within the top group, the very wealthiest did best of all. Those in the top 5 percent saw increases of 37.3 percent, while those in the top 1 percent had gains of almost 75 percent. Looking at dollar amounts rather than percentage of increase, the report found that in 1988 average family income in the lowest 10 percent was $3157, while average family income in the highest 10 percent was $124,651, and in the highest 1 percent, the average was $303,900.[2]

The utilitarian argument about the marginal utility of money strongly suggests that this kind of distribution does not maximize human well-being. We could increase the total well-being of people by redistributing some of this money. We could do this because the loss of money for the wealthy would have little if any negative impact on their well-being, while the gains for the poor would be significant.

If this is correct, it supports the socialist's case in two ways. First, it undermines the optimistic picture that defenders of capitalism give. Even if capitalism is the most productive system, it permits a distribution that causes some to live in misery while others have vast resources that do them little good.

Second, from a utilitarian point of view, if the right act or policy is the one that maximizes utility or well-being, then some form of distribution of resources by the state would seem to be morally required. Instead of leaving distribution to market forces, socialists argue that a better distribution and more utility can be achieved by consciously allocating resources in accord with people's needs. It would be better to have some central process that directs resources to the people who can get the most out of them, rather than allowing for the cumulative growth of wealth among those who already possess more than they need.

DOES CAPITALISM REWARD THE DESERVING?

As we saw earlier, defenders of capitalism sometimes appeal to the idea that it best satisfies our desire that people should be paid in proportion to what they deserve. Those who work hard or make significant contributions should be paid more than people who are lazy or unproductive.

[2] "The 1980's: A Very Good Time for the Very Rich," *New York Times*, March 5, 1992, p. 1.

Hard work and the production of valuable things sometimes do have these effects in a capitalist economy. Nonetheless, it is clear that they are not major factors in determining the distribution of wealth. John Stuart Mill, reflecting on this issue, put his conclusion bluntly. Commenting on the workings of capitalism in his own time, he wrote,

> The very idea of distributive justice, or of any proportionality between success and merit, or between success and exertion, is in the present state of society so manifestly chimerical as to be relegated to the regions of romance.[3]

While Mill's conclusion runs counter to much popular belief, reflection on the workings of a market economy makes it very plausible. That a capitalist system rewards desert appears to be more a matter of myth than reality.

One reason for this has already emerged in my discussion of growing disparities in wealth. This is the continuing influence of previous economic successes and failures. People who succeed and have a lot of money can continue to earn a great deal simply by investing their money and earning interest, dividends, and profits from the sale of stocks or real estate. Such people need not work at all. Marx and Engels made this point in exaggerated form in *The Communist Manifesto*, asserting that in a capitalist society, "those of its members who work, acquire nothing, and those who acquire anything, do not work"[4].

Moreover, if people are permitted to pass on inheritances to their children, then the fruits of past success can be made relatively permanent, ensuring that new generations will flourish economically without any effort or contribution at all. Since no one deserves to be born into a particular family, no one can deserve to receive an inheritance. This means that no society in which inheritance is an important source of wealth will meet the ideal of rewards in accord with desert.[5]

A similar conclusion about the failure of capitalism to reward hard work follows from considering the factors that determine salary levels. People with few skills must compete with many others for jobs, and this has the effect of lowering the wages for unskilled work, even if that work requires much effort. Migrant agricultural workers, coal miners, and factory workers often work longer hours under more adverse conditions than many people who earn much more than they do.

Nor does a greater contribution to others ensure greater compensation. Recall Tom Cottle's protest about the earnings of school teachers like his wife in relation to the earnings of baseball players. Commenting on the practice by which baseball players can earn additional money by signing autographs, Cottle notes, "By writing their names, ballplayers may receive a financial bonus. My wife teaches children how to write their names."[6] Surely, giving children the skill to write and communicate makes a more valuable contribu-

[3] J.S. Mill, *On Socialism* (Buffalo, N.Y.: Prometheus Books, 1987), 70.

[4] Marx and Engels, 70.

[5] For a criticism of inheritance and a proposal to limit it severely, see D.W. Haslett, *Capitalism With Morality*. (New York: Oxford University Press, 1995), chap. 6.

[6] Tom Cottle, "Throwing a Curve at Our Teachers," *Boston Sunday Globe, Focus Section*, January 7, 1990.

tion to their lives than giving signed baseball cards makes to the lives of collectors. Yet, it need not lead to greater compensation in a market system.

There are, of course, explanations for why pay is not proportional to the value of an activity. In this case, the fame of baseball players gives their signatures on cards a resale value that is likely to increase over the years. Teachers' salaries are relatively low because they are paid from public funds, their productivity cannot be vastly increased, and there is apparently a large enough pool of people who are willing to work as teachers in spite of the relatively low pay.[7]

To explain these economic results is not the same as justifying them, however. Moreover, even if we decide that the relative salaries of baseball players and teachers are justified, we could only reach that conclusion by abandoning the criterion of moral desert. Suppose, for example, that we accept the view that a market economy is simply the best one, even though one feature of such an economy is that athletes and entertainers can make vast amounts of money, while school teachers make very relatively little. Even if this view is correct, it is clearly inconsistent with the ideal of giving people what they deserve. Anyone who accepts this view must admit that they have forsaken the demand that resources be distributed in accord with effort, contribution, or other measures of personal desert.

Many of capitalism's sophisticated defenders accept this logic and support capitalism, while acknowledging that it does not reward desert. Robert Nozick, for example, says that while we feel more comfortable about "the justice of an entitlement system if most of the transfers under it are done for reasons, . . . [t]his does not mean necessarily that all deserve what holdings they receive."[8] In fact, a system of reward in accord with desert is precisely the kind of "patterned" criterion of justice that Nozick opposes. For him, the essence of a just system is that transfers are made voluntarily. Whether resources go to people who are deserving is entirely irrelevant. This emerges most clearly in Nozick's defense of inheritance. He argues that the practice of inheritance is justified not because the recipients deserve what they get but rather because donors are entitled to give their money away to others if they wish.

Likewise, Milton Friedman does not claim that a market system rewards moral desert. In fact, he says,

> Most differences of status or position or wealth can be regarded as the product of chance at a far enough remove.[9]

And F. A. Hayek laments the fact that some advocates of capitalism ever tried to establish its superiority by appeal to desert. He writes:

[7] For a discussion of the factors that influence the salaries of teachers and other professionals, see Derek Bok, *The Cost of Talent* (New York: The Free Press, 1993).

[8] Robert Nozick, *Anarchy, State and Utopia* (New York: Basic Books, 1973), 159.

[9] Milton Friedman, *Capitalism and Freedom* (Chicago: University of Chicago Press, 1962), 165–66.

> It is probably a misfortune that, especially in the USA, popular writers . . . have defended free enterprise on the ground that it regularly rewards the deserving, and it bodes ill for the future of the market order that this seems to have become the only defence of it which is understood by the general public.[10]

Hayek's remark is interesting because it acknowledges the existence of a widespread desire that rewards be distributed in accord with desert. He admits, however, that this is an ideal that a market economy does not aim for and is unlikely to realize.

SOCIALISM AND DESERT

While socialists may effectively criticize capitalism for failing to distribute goods in accord with desert, it does not follow that socialism would succeed in doing so. In fact, it is not clear that socialists favor this ideal themselves. The main distributive ideals in socialism are need and equality. For this reason, socialists would not want substantially more goods to be distributed to people who work harder or contribute more. That would violate their egalitarian ideals and the priority they give to meeting needs.

Given this conflict, socialists can adopt either of two views about the ideal of distribution according to desert. Either they can retain the ideal of giving people what they deserve, while offering a different interpretation of what this means, or they can retain the traditional concept of desert, while giving it either no role or a much reduced role in determining how goods should be distributed.

Let us consider the first view, which retains the ideal of basing distribution on desert. A socialist could claim that when this view is properly interpreted, it supports the socialist ideal that goods should be distributed more or less equally. Thomas Nagel suggests this view when he writes that

> differential abilities are not usually among the characteristics that determine whether people *deserve* economic and social benefits (though of course they determine whether people *get* such benefits). In fact, I believe that nearly all characteristics are irrelevant to what people deserve in this dimension, and that most people therefore deserve to be treated equally. . . . I do not have a precise view about what features are relevant. I contend only that they are features in which most people do not differ enough to justify very wide differences in reward.[11]

While Nagel's views about desert are not fully developed, his remarks contain ideas that are in harmony with socialist ideals. First, he believes that "wide differences in reward" cannot be justified by appeal to desert. This fits in with the socialist's emphasis on equality. Second, he believes that the fea-

[10] F.A. Hayek, *The Mirage of Social Justice,* Volume 2 of *Law, Legislation, and Liberty* (London: Routledge and Kegan Paul, 1976), 74.

[11] Thomas Nagel, "Equal Treatment and Compensatory Discrimination," *Philosophy & Public Affairs* 2 (1973), 354.

tures that determine the level of resources people deserve are features "in which most people do not differ" substantially. Since most people do not differ substantially in their basic needs, if needs (rather than achievement) were the basis of desert, a relatively egalitarian distribution would give people what they deserve.

Suppose, then, that what people deserve is determined in large part by their needs and that most people's needs do not differ substantially enough to warrant wide discrepancies in allocation. In that case, we could give people what they deserve by providing a roughly equal distribution of goods. This is precisely what socialists argue for.[12]

If we accept this argument, we must come to believe that there is more than one concept of "desert." The concept that we considered earlier focuses on people's individual efforts or achievements. It is a concept of *personal* desert. Nagel's remarks suggest that there is another kind of desert that belongs to us simply by virtue of our humanity. For this reason, I will call it *human* desert.[13] Unlike personal desert, which is possessed in varying degrees by individuals and depends on what they have done, human desert is based on features we all share and is possessed equally by all human beings. This notion of human desert is related to the idea of basic human rights, which are moral claims that people have simply by virtue of their humanity. They are rights that no one has to earn.

Since socialists believe that all human beings have a basic right to a share of the social product, Nagel's reflections provide a useful basis for their view. Building on Nagel's points, a socialist could claim that the distribution of goods should be based on *human* desert rather than *personal* desert. Moreover, while some rewards might be distributed on the basis of personal desert, these would not be substantial enough to create large disparities in income and well-being.

Someone might object that the only kind of desert is personal desert and that the concept of human desert makes no sense. Faced with this objection, socialists might adopt a second view. They might simply reject the criterion of desert altogether and claim that what people deserve is irrelevant to the fundamental issues of how goods should be distributed. What is relevant is the moral priority of meeting people's needs and the egalitarian ideal of treating all people (at least roughly) equally. Even if some people deserve a greater share of goods by virtue of their efforts or achievements, their degree of desert could never be so great as to justify a distribution in which some flourish in unbounded luxury while others lack the basic necessities of life. Personal desert, according to socialists, should at most play a small role in determining the size of the social product that people may justly claim.

[12] If people's needs vary greatly, then "to each, according to their needs" will not support a simple, equal distribution policy. This is a problem that socialists need to face.

[13] Alan Zaitchik uses the term "automatic desert" to make a similar point in "Deserving to Deserve." *Philosophy and Public Affairs*, 6 (1977), 371–88. See also, Amy Gutman, *Liberal Equality* (Princeton, N.J.: Princeton University Press), 166–67.

The socialist perspective on desert, then, contains two parts. The negative part attempts to show that capitalism cannot justify the claim that it actually succeeds in rewarding desert. The positive claim is that if desert is to provide a basis for distributing goods, it needs to be either reconceived (so that all people end up being roughly equally deserving) or given a minimal role in the distribution of goods. Either way, needs and equality are the dominant distributive concepts for socialists, not rewards in proportion to merit or desert.

CAPITALISM, SOCIALISM, AND INDIVIDUAL LIBERTY

Recall that the third main argument for capitalism is that it respects people's liberty and thereby protects us against intrusive, oppressive government activities. In a libertarian capitalist order, people have a right to do whatever they want with their resources. They are free to engage in a range of voluntary transfers, including buying and selling, gift giving, charity, and the bequeathing of inheritances. Moreover, as in the example of Wilt Chamberlain, people can negotiate arrangements that result in some possessing much more than others. Nozick and other defenders of libertarian capitalism believe that any attempt to prohibit inequalities or prevent the accumulation of great wealth will lead to continuous interference in people's lives. Moreover, the use of taxation to help some people meet their needs will violate other people's right to do what they want with the resources they possess. Taxation is a forced transfer, not a voluntary one, and therefore, taxing to provide "welfare" assistance to others limits the liberty of people to use their resources as they personally think is best.

Libertarians, then, see themselves as defending individual liberty from the encroachment of coercive government institutions. Echoing a famous line from Thoreau, they believe that "that government is best, which governs least," and they seek to restrict the role of government to that of a minimal state, a state that prevents force and fraud but otherwise leaves people alone.[14] On their view, as long as people are not directly harming one another, they should be free to do what they want.

The socialist criticism of this view begins with the complaint that the libertarian conception of freedom is too narrow. Socialists understand freedom as something positive. It is the ability to act. Libertarian defenders of capitalism, however, think of freedom in a negative sense. For them, people are free if they are not interfered with by other people. As long as no one is coercing me to do something I don't want to do or preventing me from doing what I do want to do, then I am free.

The difference between positive and negative conceptions of freedom is extremely important. For socialists, a person has the freedom to eat a meal, for example, if she possesses food, has the ability and utensils to prepare it

[14] H.D. Thoreau, "Civil Disobedience," in *Walden and Other Writings* (New York: Modern Library, 1937), 635.

for eating, and can actually eat it. For libertarians, a person is free to eat a meal if no one prevents her from eating. According to the libertarian view, a person who has no food and no money to buy food has the freedom to eat a meal in spite of the fact that she lacks the resources to do so. As long as no one prevents her from eating, she is free to do so, even though her lack of food makes this impossible.

According to libertarians, in a capitalist society everyone is equally free to use or exchange resources. It does not matter that some people have resources to exchange while others do not. All are equally free. Socialists see this kind of freedom as purely formal, empty, and abstract because it is totally disconnected from the actual ability to use or transfer resources.

For socialists, then, a society of free people is not simply one in which neither government nor individuals actively prevent people from doing what they want. Instead, it is a society in which people have the resources that are necessary for doing what they seek to do. To be free to do something is to have the power to do it. People's freedom is proportional to their power, and their power is often proportional to the resources they possess.

From the socialist perspective, a capitalist society fails to provide equal liberty for all its citizens. It fails to do so because it permits vast inequalities in resources, and inequalities in resources create inequalities in liberty.

HOW LIBERTY UPSETS LIBERTY

Nozick contrasts the libertarian "procedural" conception of justice with what he calls "patterned" conceptions of justice. An egalitarian socialist ideal, for example, is patterned because it seeks to make the distribution of resources conform to some ideal pattern of distribution. For egalitarian socialists, the ideal pattern is achieved when everyone has the same amount of resources.

Nozick argues that respecting people's liberty necessarily undermines any patterned conception of justice. If government simply lets people exchange resources freely, there is little chance that any particular pattern of distribution will result. Hence, if socialists or others want to impose a patterned distribution, that will require them to interfere with people's liberty.

In drawing this conclusion, Nozick is certainly correct. A government that tries to implement an ideal pattern of distribution will have to prohibit departures from that pattern, and, as Nozick forcefully brings out, it will have to prohibit someone like Wilt Chamberlain from obtaining more money than others, even if others are willing to pay extra to see him play basketball.

Nonetheless, what Nozick's argument overlooks is that liberty itself can undermine liberty. In a libertarian capitalist society, people with resources can engage in any transactions they want. As a result, people without resources must live with significant limitations on their liberty. For example, children born to poor families will not be free to obtain the education required for developing their mental capacities or the nutrition and health care required to develop their physical capacities. The freedom of an unconstrained market economy results in a lack of freedom for poor children and prevents them from equipping themselves to compete effectively in a market economy. Likewise, the freedom of wealthy people to leave inheritances to their children limits the freedom of poorer children to compete on an equal basis for education and jobs.

If advantages in a market economy tend to be cumulative, then granting people the right to absolute control over their property will mean that, over time, the freedom of some will continue to increase, while the freedom of others will decrease. Growing disparities of income and wealth will be matched by growing disparities of freedom.

People in poverty with few skills are not free to turn down jobs that involve long hours, unhealthy working conditions, and low pay. They are forced to take such jobs because they lack alternative opportunities and because this is the only way they can earn a living. Of course, they are *legally* free to turn down such jobs. No one tells them that if they do not take them, they will be subject to legal punishment. Nonetheless, they are in no position to take advantage of the *formal* right to decline such a job.

Socialists believe that a system that guarantees people equal shares of the social product would produce a vast increase in freedom, since many people would gain the resources to make a larger selection of actions possible. To achieve this would require taking away the liberty to accumulate unlimited amounts of resources. At the same time, it would vastly increase the freedom to choose and act for most people.

For socialists, then, the choice is not between freedom under capitalism or oppression under socialism. The choice is between a capitalist system that provides formal freedom for all and actual freedom for only some and a socialist system in which limits on the freedom to accumulate wealth create vastly increased positive freedom for most people.

THE CASE FOR SOCIALISM

The socialist argument, then, has two main parts: a critique of capitalism and a defense of the socialist alternative. The two parts are related, however, for each of the criticisms of capitalism suggests that the socialist alternative could solve the problem that capitalism creates or permits.

Contrary to what capitalists have argued, socialists claim that their system would distribute goods in a way that maximizes their usefulness in promoting human well-being. In their view, the diminishing marginal utility of wealth and the tendency of capitalism to produce disparities of wealth show that a roughly equal distribution would produce the highest overall level of human well-being. Capitalism wastes too many resources on people whose needs are already satisfied, while socialism channels resources in ways that will do the most good.

Second, while socialists reject the idea that some people deserve much more than others, they accept the idea that all people should get what is due to them. Unlike capitalists, they think that what people deserve or are entitled to is a roughly equal share of the social product. If each person's life is important and valuable in its own right, then giving people their due requires attending to their needs. Capitalism, socialists say, fails to do this. It neglects the needs of many in order to protect the right of a minority to control large-scale resources. Socialism, however, gives the satisfaction of needs the highest priority in the use of resources.

Finally, while capitalism is often defended as a bulwark of freedom, socialists argue that it protects only negative or formal freedom; it does nothing to protect positive freedom, the actual ability of people to act in pursuit of their goals. Since real freedom varies with the resources available to people, socialism maximizes freedom by spreading resources around. Socialism permits people to be genuinely free because it makes sure they have the resources they need to act according to their own desires and decisions.

This does not mean that everyone can do everything they want. What we can do is limited by our abilities, by limits on the resources available to society, and by limits on our legitimate claim to resources. What socialism strives to give everyone, however, is a roughly equal share of social resources, and this means that by and large, any one person's ability to act on his own decisions will be as extensive as the ability of any other person to do so.

SUMMING UP

Socialists acknowledge the great productive powers that capitalism has helped to develop. They also grant the value of the goals that capitalists often cite as the justification for their system: making people as well off as possible, giving everyone his or her proper due, and making people as free as possible.

Nonetheless, socialists argue, capitalism fails to distribute the benefits of its productive capacity in ways that achieve these goals. These goals, socialists claim, can only be met if they are made the explicit aim of government policy. They will never be met if they are left to the workings of the market economy. If people who cite these goals are serious, they will be forced to embrace socialism rather than capitalism.

CHAPTER FIVE

Promoting Well-Being

ASSESSING CAPITALISM AND SOCIALISM

In Part I, I described some of the arguments that advocates of capitalism and socialism use to promote their views. While the case for capitalism contains some strong arguments, the socialist case against capitalism also has considerable force. Faced with these socialist criticisms, advocates of capitalism have come to its defense, trying to rebut objections and establish capitalism's superiority. As with all complex issues, the debate between capitalism and socialism contains points and counterpoints, objections and replies, replies to replies, and so on.

At some point, however, we need to try to resolve the issues, even if our conclusions are only tentative. In this and the next two chapters, I try to reach such a resolution by evaluating both systems from the perspective of the three values that are so central to our thinking about economic justice: human well-being, rewards for the deserving, and the enhancement of liberty. Each system claims to be superior with respect to these values. Now that we have seen how defenders of both views appeal to these values, we can assess how successful they are. In doing so, we can also see how defenders of the welfare state enter the debate and why they think that a welfare state system is superior to both capitalism and socialism.

THE UTILITARIAN ARGUMENT

Advocates of both capitalism and socialism claim that their system is right or just because it best promotes human well-being. This is, in effect, a utilitarian argument, since utilitarianism identifies what is right to do with what best promotes well-being. Even if it is a mistake to identify moral rightness or justice with the production of well-being, it remains true that a system that shows itself to be the best promoter of well-being will have a powerful argument in its favor. People rightly judge economic systems by their results, and one crucial result is how well off or badly off they make people's lives.

To this point, we have seen two main arguments for the view that capitalism makes people best off—an appeal to history and an abstract argument about the ways in which a market economy provides incentives for productivity. The historical argument compares the levels of well-being in capitalist and socialist countries and reminds us that formerly socialist countries are turning increasingly to capitalism. The abstract argument describes the ways in which a competitive economy gives people both positive and negative incentives to produce goods that enhance human life.

Socialists have their own account of history. It stresses the costs of capitalism in human terms, the harm produced by cycles of boom and bust, and most of all, the fact that the benefits of capitalist production reach only some people, while others live in poverty. Likewise, they note the disadvantages that some socialist countries began under and their success in promoting economic growth and industrial development.[1]

Socialists argue that capitalism in inherently inefficient. It fails to promote human well-being effectively because it permits vast amounts of resources to be channeled to people who already have them. When these resources go to people who are already well off, they exhibit diminished marginal utility; they do less good for the well off than they would for the poor. Socialists argue that we can maximize the value of resources by adopting a more equalized distribution. We can maximize utility by taking from the rich (because diminishing their resources won't really harm them) and giving more to the poor (since those same resources will bring substantial improvements in well-being).

From the socialist perspective, capitalism is wasteful and inefficient because it permits the concentration of resources in a small part of the population. Socialism, they claim, would effectively promote well-being by distributing resources in accord with principles of need and value.

THE CAPITALIST REPLY TO THE MARGINAL UTILITY ARGUMENT

Capitalists reject this argument and claim that it involves a fundamental mistake. Socialists assume that we could have the productivity of capitalism without the unequal distribution that capitalism generates. According to advocates of capitalism, this is a serious error. They argue that the productivity of

[1] For comparisons of different economic systems from a point of view that is sympathetic to capitalism, see Peter Berger, *The Capitalist Revolution* (New York: Basic Books, 1986). For a survey of issues from a socialist perspective, see Tom Bottomore, *The Socialist Economy: Theory and Practice* (New York: Guilford Press, 1990). For an overview by an economist, see Gregory Grossman, *Economic Systems*, 2nd ed. (Englewood Cliffs, N.J.: Prentice Hall, 1974).

the capitalist system is closely linked to the unequal rewards that result from it. You cannot tamper with the distribution system, they say, without destroying capitalism's high productivity.

Why is this? Because high productivity is the direct result of the incentives for individuals to be productive. People have an incentive to produce better products and services because if they succeed, they can increase their earnings and acquire greater benefits for themselves, their families, and others they care about. If people work hard and succeed in producing valuable goods and services, they themselves will benefit directly from their success. They will benefit by having more money to purchase the goods that money can buy, whether those goods be luxuries or necessities.

In addition, if people accumulate more money than is necessary to meet their needs and satisfy their desires, they can invest their money in ways that will generate new or better productive enterprises. These investments will gain more benefits for themselves while at the same time playing an important role in the growth of the economy.

If people could not benefit themselves in these ways, they would lack the incentive to be productive. In an egalitarian socialist system, no matter how hard people work or how much they produce, they themselves can earn no more than someone who does not work hard and is unproductive. Without the prospect of personal benefit, there would be much less motivation to work hard, to be innovative, and to contribute to increased productivity.

This point can be strengthened by recalling that much of the work needed by a society is difficult and unpleasant. If people are to be motivated to perform this work, they must be able to benefit personally by increasing their own rewards or by preventing themselves from the suffering of economic deprivation. A capitalist economy works by "sticks" as well as "carrots," providing both positive and negative incentives to work. People work hard to get what they desire *and* to avoid what they justifiably fear—hunger, lack of shelter, and the loss of goods that make survival possible and life pleasant.

Looked at realistically, capitalists claim, a market economy is necessary for high productivity. It makes effective use of the powerful motives of fear and desire. Without these, people would simply work less hard, and society as a whole would be less productive.

If everyone were guaranteed an equal share of the social product, the incentives to work would diminish and productivity would decline. In a socialist economy, the sum total of goods would be much smaller, and the economy would not be productive enough to provide everyone with a decent standard of living. Greater equality would be achieved, but the mass of people would be worse off than they are in a capitalist economy. The poor would still be poor, and those who had enjoyed a good life under capitalism no longer would do so.

The crucial flaw in the socialist case, then, is that it treats production and distribution as separate matters. In fact, capitalists argue, it is the system of unequal rewards that makes capitalism so productive. Take away the possibility of rich rewards for the successful and the possibility of dire poverty for those who do not work, and you take away the possibility of high productivity. The socialist vision of a highly productive, egalitarian society rests on a delusion.

ARE THERE OTHER MOTIVATIONS?

In order to reply to the argument that productivity will fall drastically in the absence of unequal rewards, socialists need an alternative theory of motivation. This is especially important because socialists want to create a world in which people are secure enough to be free of fear and content enough not to want more goods than others. They need to explain why people will work hard if doing so will not benefit them personally and if failing to work will not deprive them of anything.

What socialists claim is that defenders of capitalism are themselves making unwarranted assumptions both about human motivation and about work. Capitalists assume that people are lazy and self-centered and therefore that they will only work if prodded by sticks or induced by carrots. Likewise, they assume that work is inherently repulsive so that external inducements to work will always be necessary. While these assumptions may be true in a capitalist society, they will not be true in a socialist society.

In a socialist society, they argue, people will be different, and work will be different. Freed from competition and the struggle to survive in a capitalist society, people's social tendencies will become more highly developed and their need to act self-interestedly will diminish. Likewise, work itself will change. It will be organized so as to minimize drudgery and will not be seen as a badge of low status. Rather, work will become a means for people to realize themselves in a productive, satisfying activity.

Marx explicitly recognized that many changes would be necessary before an ideal socialist society could be achieved. Only after these changes had occurred could the socialist ideal of distribution according to need be met. The highest, most ideal phase of "communism" would only be reached, he wrote,

> after the enslaving subordination of individuals under division of labor, and therewith also the antithesis between mental and physical labour, has vanished; after labour, from a mere means of life, has itself become the prime necessity of life; after the productive forces have also increased with the all-round development of the individual, and all the springs of co-operative wealth flow more abundantly—only then can the narrow horizon of bourgeois right be fully left behind and society inscribe on its banners: from each according to his ability, to each according to his needs![2]

Contrary, then, to the claim that socialists ignore the connection between production and distribution, Marx argues that in order to achieve a socialist

[2] Karl Marx, *Critique of the Gotha Program* (New York: International Publishers, 1938), 10.

distribution, the conditions of production and the incentives for work must be thoroughly transformed. Only when people have changed so that they willingly work according to their ability can the ideal of distribution according to need by realized.

While Marx's comments show an awareness of the problem of incentives for work, they may unwittingly suggest that the problem is impossible to solve. For socialism to succeed, people's motivations must be different, but for people's motivations to be different, they must inhabit a different social system. This looks like a vicious circle, however. The move from capitalism to socialism seems to require motivations in people that will only come to exist when socialism is already in place.

Marx's solution to this problem is that the move from capitalism to full socialism must take place in stages. "From each according to his ability, to each according to his needs" can be achieved only in the final, highest stage of a communist society. It is not to be expected as the immediate result of the overthrow of capitalism. During the first, "lower" stage of socialism, a different system will have to operate, one that makes work a necessity. In this first stage, Marx writes,

> the individual producer receives back from society . . . exactly what he gives to it. . . . He receives a certificate from society that he has furnished such and such an amount of labour (after deducting his labour for the common fund), and with this certificate he draws from the social stock of means of consumption as much as the same amount of labour costs. The same amount of labour which he has given to society in one form, he receives back in another.[3]

At this stage, then, people must work in order to receive the goods needed for living, and the amount of goods people receive is strictly proportional to the amount of work they do.

Marx does not describe how to get from this stage to the full socialist ideal. Presumably he believed that over time, as public ownership takes effect, as the distribution of wealth is roughly equalized in society, and as conditions of work improve, people will cease to strive for themselves alone. The effects of the socialization process that prepared people for life under capitalism will wither away, and they will develop a set of motivations that are compatible with socialism.

BACK TO THE PRESENT

Is Marx's answer to the incentive problem adequate?

Defenders of capitalism are likely to think that human nature is inherently self-centered in ways that make his vision implausible. Even thinkers who are sympathetic with socialist ideals have felt doubts about its demands on altruistic motivation. John Stuart Mill, after reflecting on this problem, concluded that

[3] Ibid., 8.

> the motive of conscience and that of credit and reputation . . . are more to be depended on for preventing wrong, than for calling forth the fullest energies in the pursuit of ordinary occupations. In the case of most men the only inducement which has been found sufficiently constant and unflagging to overcome the ever-present influence of indolence and love of ease, and induce men to apply themselves unrelaxingly to work for the most part in itself dull and unexciting, is the prospect of bettering their own economic condition and that of their family; and the closer the connection of every increase of exertion with a corresponding increase of its fruits, the more powerful is its motive.[4]

Similarly, Thomas Nagel, having defended economic egalitarianism on ethical grounds, argues that an egalitarian economic system is incompatible with human nature. He writes:

> It is psychologically difficult to realize a decent social ideal with real people, as opposed to characters in utopian fiction . . . . [I]t does not belong to the socialized nature of modern man in general to be motivated by a concern for the good of all in most of his working, let alone private, life. . . . [T]he result is that the most successful economies are competitive and give rise to substantial inequalities, which inevitably get passed on from generation to generation.[5]

The fact that both these quotes come from thinkers who are highly sympathetic with socialist aims suggests that we need to take seriously the possibility that socialism presupposes a false psychology.

To take this claim seriously, however, is not the same as accepting it as an obvious truth. Marx's more optimistic assessment is neither foolish nor obviously wrong. Human nature is both variable and malleable in many respects. After all, people throughout the world are socialized into different cultures, and we can see the profound differences between members of distinct cultures. They differ in customs and tastes, as well as in their sense of what is important and worth striving for. Nor are people always predominantly self-seeking. The willingness of people to risk their lives for their country shows that even strong natural inclinations toward self-preservation can be overcome by socialization processes, psychic rewards, and public pressure. Less dramatically, many people contribute freely to charity and volunteer their time and effort to assist others. Moreover, the possibility of altering people's motivations is supported by the effects of advertising. Advertising seems capable of producing entirely new and very powerful desires in people for certain kinds of products.

All these phenomena suggest that people might be able to live and work productively within a socialist value scheme. It is not at all absurd to believe that people would be less competitive and less self-interested if they lived in a world in which they were both more secure and better provided for by their society. In such a world, they might well acquire motivations to work

[4] Mill, *On Socialism*, (Buffalo: Prometheus Books, 1987), 120.

[5] Thomas Nagel, *Equality and Partiality* (New York: Oxford University Press, 1991), 93.

that are independent of the fear and desire that motivate work in a capitalist society.[6]

Still, for the foreseeable future, competitive and self-seeking motivations, along with the heightened concern that most people feel for their own families and friends, will remain powerful obstacles to achieving a socialist society.

THE WELFARE STATE SOLUTION

The clash of capitalists and socialists on this issue appears to present us with a dilemma. If we choose capitalism, we have a better chance that our economy will be sufficiently productive to make everyone well off, but the system of unequal rewards will leave some people very badly off, while others will have much more than they need. If we choose socialism, we will have an equitable distribution, but the economy seems less likely to produce enough to provide everyone with a decent standard of living.

Capitalists conclude that the best we can do is to have an economy that provides a good life for some. In their more high spirited moments, they may claim that the good life can be achieved by all who are willing to work. When they are being more honest, they acknowledge that the suffering of many may be an inevitable part of the system. Socialists reject the inevitability of poverty, but they grant that changing the system requires people to be differently motivated and that this can only occur when the new system has already taken root.

Advocates of the welfare state deny that our choice is this bleak. They think we can have the best of both worlds—high productivity and a somewhat more equitable distribution. Their idea is a simple one. If some portion of people's assets is collected in taxes and used to assist people in need, this will not diminish the incentive to work because those who are taxed will still be better off than they would have been if they had not worked. More work will still lead to greater rewards, even if the entire earnings are not kept. If too much is taken, of course, people may come to think that their extra efforts are not worth making, but if the tax rate is set properly, it will collect some money from the better off to aid those in need, while still leaving intact the incentives that motivate increased productivity.

The welfare state provides the utilitarian solution to the problem. It does this by rejecting aspects of both the capitalist and the socialist positions. It rejects the libertarian capitalist's extreme claim that people must retain all their economic earnings if the incentive to be more productive is to operate. Instead, its defenders claim, some loss in taxes is compatible with sustained incentives for greater rewards. Likewise, the welfare state solution rejects the idea that only fear of hunger and death will cause people at the lower

[6] For two visions of what a socialist society would look like that differ both from Marx and from one another, see Edward Bellamy, *Looking Backward*, and William Morris, *News from Nowhere*, (London: Rutledge & Kegan Paul, 1970). Bellamy's ideas are further developed in *Equality*, *(New York: Appleton, 1897).*

end of the economic ladder to work. Advocates of the welfare state think that poor people will still have an incentive to work even if their basic needs are met. They will have this incentive because increased earnings will still enable them to make their lives more pleasant and worthwhile.

The welfare state solution also rejects the socialist's commitment to the goal of equality. It does this because it accepts the capitalist argument that economic equality would lead to diminished productivity. Economic equality is a self-defeating goal because it would probably make everyone worse off. Nor is equality inherently important from a utilitarian point of view. What is important is preventing needless suffering and making people as well off as possible. Whether or not all are equally well off is irrelevant.

If an equal distribution of resources would lead to the highest total of well-being, then it would be worth striving for. But equality itself has no inherent value. From a utilitarian point of view, inequality is only wrong if it produces unnecessary suffering. If inequality is necessary to fuel the economy, making it productive enough to provide a decent standard of living for all, then there is nothing the matter with that inequality.

This anti-egalitarian argument is related to what John Rawls calls the "difference principle." According to Rawls, inequalities are justified if they improve the situation of all and in particular if they improve the lot of the least well off. His reasoning shows why equality drops out as a substantive value. Suppose that you could choose between two situations. In situation A, everyone earns $1000 per year, enough for a meager and hard existence. In situation B, some people may earn $2000 per year provided that their doing so yields enough added production to raise everyone to a minimum of $1250.

	Situation A	**Situation B**
Person 1	$1000	$1250
Person 2	1000	1250
Person 3	1000	2000

Certainly if we are utilitarians and want to make people as well off as possible, we would choose B instead of A. Likewise, if you or I were choosing a situation for ourselves, it would seem irrational to choose A rather than B, since no matter what position we occupy, we will be better off in B than in A.

The point of this argument is that we should not attach an exaggerated value to the goal of equality. It is well-being that matters, not equality, and if permitting inequalities increases well-being, then we should do so. After all, the real concern of socialists should be the positive goal of making everyone better off, not the negative goal of preventing anyone from being better off than anyone else.

A similar argument shows that defenders of capitalism are wrong to insist that taxation necessarily destroys the incentive to be more productive. Consider the following choice.

	Situation A	Situation B	Situation C
Person 1	$1000	$1250	$1300
Person 2	1000	1250	1300
Person 3	1000	2000	2500

If we accept the capitalist view that incentives must be unlimited to promote productivity, that would require us to believe that Person 3 would have a strong incentive to move from A ($1000) to C ($2500) but would have no incentive to move from A ($1000) to B ($2000). Yet surely the improvement in moving from A to B is significant, and it is implausible to insist that only the prospect of C provides a sufficient incentive for further work.

The welfare state advocate seems to have a good argument here. Rather than dogmatically holding to a doctrine of strict equality or a doctrine that people will only be motivated if they can keep the entire fruit of their efforts, the welfarist holds two things. First, it is possible to place some limit on rewards (through taxation) without losing their ability to motivate productivity. Second, it is legitimate to allow inequality when doing so helps to increase productivity and thereby makes it possible to provide resources to everyone.

PLAYING IT BY EAR

In order to implement this sort of policy, we need to make two decisions. We need to decide, first, the amount of resources people are to receive from the state and, second, the level of taxation that can be applied without diminishing the incentives for productive work. These two decisions are related, for the amount of resources available for the state to distribute depends on the overall productivity of the society, and the productivity of the society depends partly on the size of the economic rewards available to people who produce more.

These decisions can only be made experimentally on the basis of information about motivations and incentives. One could figure out the costs of various "welfare programs" (such as food stamps, public education, unemployment insurance) and then devise a tax code that can produce the needed revenues. While at first one might have to make some guesses, over time it might become clear that while a certain level of taxation does not diminish incentives or productivity, a higher level does. What the exact level is cannot be known in advance. To make matters more complicated, the answer to this question may vary in different societies and may even vary over time in a single society. There is no abstract formula to settle this matter, and a utilitarian welfarist will support playing it by ear, raising and lowering both the tax rates and the amount of welfare state provisions offered to citizens in whatever way is required to do the most good.

THE LIMITS ON UTILITARIAN ARGUMENTS

Utilitarian arguments are an important part of moral reasoning. Capitalists, socialists, and welfare state advocates are all happy to claim that their system will do the best job of maximizing human well-being. They are also happy to claim that the systems of their adversaries will diminish people's level of well-being. Of course, which systems actually have which effects is an empirical matter. By itself, the utilitarian ideal of maximizing well-being does not tell us what to do. It only leads to practical conclusions when it is linked to empirical beliefs about the most likely effects of doing one thing rather than another. That is why factual beliefs about how various systems will affect incentives and productivity play such a central role in these debates.

While most people are happy to appeal to utilitarian arguments when they support their favored views, most of us are not strict utilitarians, and it is worth noting that utilitarian arguments about distribution might support conclusions that are not plausible. To see this, consider another choice.

	Situation A	**Situation B**
Person 1	$1000	$250
Person 2	1000	250
Person 3	1000	3000

In this case, we can maximize the total amount of well-being by moving from A to B, but we do so at the cost of making persons 1 and 2 significantly worse off. So, if we are utilitarians and care only about total well-being, we will prefer B to A. Yet, this conclusion scarcely seems correct if we are concerned about justice. The preference for B seems to show a lack of concern for persons 1 and 2 and neglects the question of what a person's fair share is. Whatever problems may exist with the ideal of equality, it at least permits us to condemn the move from A to B as an injustice. A pure utilitarian theory does not even permit doubts about the preferability of B over A because it is concerned only with total well-being and not directly with the way in which well-being is distributed among different people.

Again, this is not to deny that utilitarian reasoning is an important aspect of our deliberations. This example, however, shows that it is not the whole story.

SUMMING UP

In this chapter, I have considered utilitarian arguments for and against both capitalism and socialism. I have tried to show that the best solution to the problems raised is provided neither by pure capitalism nor by pure socialism. The best solution is provided by advocates of a welfare state.

Welfare statists reject capitalism's allocation criterion: to each according to market value plus gifts. They reject this criterion because it leads to a maldistribution of resources that fails to do the most good. More good can be done by distributing some goods to people apart from their ability to compete in the market or to gain charity from the wealthy. This is not to say that distribution through the market or gift giving should be abolished. These remain important means of distribution, but they must be supplemented by some form of legally guaranteed access to resources for all citizens.

The welfare statist accepts the socialist view that needs are important while rejecting socialism's commitment to an equal distribution or a distribution based on need alone. This is rejected because of the fear that an equal distribution would diminish the social product to the point where no one is well off. So, unlike socialists, welfare statists permit inequalities, while trying as much as possible to increase the well-being of all within society.

Even if this welfarist strategy does a better job of maximizing well-being than either capitalism or socialism, some people may continue to object to it. Advocates of capitalism may think, for example, that it is unfair to tax people's higher earnings if those people deserve what they have. Likewise, they may think it unfair for some people to receive what they do not deserve. Similarly, socialists may protest that the wealthy in a welfare state do not really deserve their additional resources.

Even if the welfare state strategy is best from a utilitarian point of view, then, we must consider other issues before concluding that the welfare state has been fully justified.

CHAPTER SIX

Rewarding the Deserving

While promoting people's well-being is important, it is not our only concern when we think about economic systems. In addition, many of us think it is important that people get what they deserve. For many of us, in fact, getting what we deserve is the essence of justice. From this perspective, an ideal world is not necessarily one in which everyone is as well off as possible. Rather, it is one in which all people get what they deserve.

To see the importance of this point, consider one of the choices discussed in Chapter 4. Suppose we are choosing between the following situations. (The numbers here represent levels of well-being.)

	Situation A	**Situation B**
Person 1	1000	250
Person 2	1000	250
Person 3	1000	3000

While a utilitarian would favor B over A because it has a higher total utility, egalitarians and adherents of Rawls's "difference principle" would reject B. Egalitarians would reject it because of the inequalities it creates, while Rawlsians would do so because the gains of person 3 seem to be achieved by worsening the situations of 1 and 2.

Both of these criticisms, however, assume that we can tell whether a distribution is just simply by looking at how much people have at a given moment. In adopting this approach, they ignore questions about *how* this distribution originated. This point is forcefully expressed by Robert Nozick. He writes:

> Most persons . . . think it relevant in assessing the justice of a situation to consider not only the distribution it embodies [at a particular time], but also how that distribution came about. If some persons are in prison for murder or war crimes, we do not say that to assess the justice of the distribution in the society we must look only at what this person has, and that person has, and that person has....We think it is relevant to ask whether someone did something so that he *deserved* to be punished, deserved to have a lower share.[1]

Nozick stresses the importance of distinguishing between what he calls "end-state" principles of justice and "historical" principles of justice. While *end-state* principles look only at the result of a set of events or processes to determine if the distribution is just, *historical* principles look at the history of how it came about.

This is important to the view that justice requires giving people what they deserve, since what people deserve often depends on what they have done. To take Nozick's example, it would be wrong to criticize a society simply because it imprisons some of its citizens. We need to know whether those people deserve to be punished, and this requires knowing the history of what they have actually done. The same point applies to issues of distributive justice. As Nozick writes,

> [P]ast circumstances or actions of people can create differential entitlements or differential deserts to things. An injustice can . . . [occur] by moving from one distribution to another . . . if it violate[s] people's entitlements or deserts; it may not fit the actual history.[2]

Returning to the choice between A and B, what Nozick shows is that we cannot tell whether a move from A to B is just or unjust without knowing how it came about.

Suppose that persons 1, 2, and 3 all began with equal shares and that 1 and 2 were lazy and self-indulgent, spending their money for parties and a good time. In contrast, suppose that person 3 used her resources to gain training or to buy equipment which then allowed her to work profitably. In this case, there may be no injustice in her having a larger share than 1 and 2. She worked and invested wisely while persons 1 and 2 did not. For this reason, she seems to deserve her larger share of resources. This is something that both utilitarians and egalitarian socialists seem to neglect.

Applying this idea to society as a whole, defenders of libertarian capitalism try to justify existing inequalities by arguing that people who work hard and contribute much should have more than others. Likewise, they appeal to desert to justify not giving aid to poor people. If people are poor because they are too lazy to work, then they do not deserve assistance. Rather, they argue, their poverty is precisely what they deserve. It is the proper "reward" for a lack of effort and contribution.

[1] Nozick, *Anarchy, State and Utopia*, 154.

[2] *Ibid.*, 155.

Defenders of capitalism use this sort of argument to show that capitalism does a better job of giving people what they deserve than either socialism or the welfare state. It does this because it pays attention to what people *do* and not simply to what they *have*.

HOW DO WE TELL WHAT PEOPLE DESERVE?

In order to decide whether a capitalist system gives people what they deserve, we need a way to determine what people do deserve.[3] In many cases in our daily life, how to determine this seems quite clear. We often make judgments about what people deserve in the context of an activity or system in which there are rules that specify the form of treatment people deserve. So, for example, the first person to cross the finish line in a race deserves the prize, while in lotteries, the deserving person is the one whose ticket is drawn. In a classroom, students who do the best work deserve to get the best grades. There are many situations like these in which we talk about people getting what they deserve and in which it is easy to tell what people deserve. When desert is based on clear rules and practices like these, I will call it "institutional" desert.

While this form of desert is very clear, it is no help in deciding whether an economic system gives people what they deserve. This is so for two reasons.

First, institutional desert *presupposes* a set of acceptable rules or practices. It helps us make judgments using those rules, but it does not tell us whether the rules themselves are morally acceptable. Before the Civil War, the legal and economic rules in the United States permitted the buying and selling of slaves. According to these rules, the person who sold a slave deserved the money he received for the sale, and the person who purchased a slave deserved to own the slave. From a purely institutional perspective, each party got what he deserved. From a moral perspective, however, neither party deserved ownership rights over the slave.

What this example shows is that we need to distinguish *institutional* desert from *moral* desert. When people say that a just economic system gives people what they deserve, they are setting up a *moral* ideal to which an economy should conform. They are not making the legalistic claim that people should get whatever the rules of their economic system call for.

This suggests a second reason why the idea of institutional desert cannot help us assess systems like capitalism and socialism. Because institutional desert is determined by the rules in force, what people deserve (in this "institutional" sense) depends entirely on what the current rules are. If a socialist society has rules that allocate an equal share to all members, then an equal share is what every member *institutionally* deserves in that society. If a capitalist society has rules that distribute resources to people according to their market value plus gifts, then what people *institutionally* deserve in that soci-

[3] In this section, I draw on ideas from my book *An Eye for an Eye?—The Immorality of Punishing by Death* (Lanham, Md.: Rowman and Littlefield, 1987), chaps. 6 and 7. For other philosophical analyses of desert, see Joel Feinberg, *Doing and Deserving* (Princeton, N.J.: Princeton University Press, 1970), and George Sher, *Desert* (Princeton, N.J.: Princeton University Press, 1987).

ety is their market value plus gifts. Institutional desert varies, making it relative to whatever system of rules happens to be in force.

If we think that a particular, existing system is unjust and fails to give people what they *really* deserve, then we must be appealing to something different from the rules of institutional desert. It is moral desert and not institutional desert that provides the standard we use to evaluate systems.

The key point here is that while institutional desert has the virtue of clarity, it cannot provide a standard for evaluating economic systems. Nor is it the ideal that people have in mind when they praise either capitalism or socialism for giving people what they deserve or denounce them for failing to do so. Each system, by living up to its own standards, automatically gives people what they *institutionally* deserve within that system, but each may nonetheless fail to give people what they morally deserve, and it is rewarding people's *moral* desert that is the aim of justice.

MORAL DESERT

What people morally deserve seems to depend on the value of their actions and not just on the rules of society or the economy. Recall Tom Cottle's protest about his wife's relatively low pay for her work as a teacher. Cottle knows the conventional rules of our society, but he thinks that they fail to reward people in accord with what they deserve. He thinks that if we reflect on what teachers do, we will see that it is unjust for them to be paid so much less than baseball players.

What is the basis of his complaint? Cottle could be arguing that teachers work harder than baseball players, that their work requires greater *effort*, and therefore that they deserve more pay than baseball players. Or, he could be arguing that the result of teachers' work, the *contribution* it makes to people's lives, is more valuable than the contribution made by baseball players and thus that they deserve more pay than baseball players. Or he could be arguing that the *abilities* required to be a good teacher are more valuable than the abilities required to play baseball and therefore merit greater pay.

These arguments might seem unjustly unappreciative of the glories of baseball. So, let me put it in a way that is less likely to offend baseball lovers. Cottle could be arguing that even if baseball players work as hard as teachers or even harder, even if they make as much or more of a contribution to people's lives than teachers, and even if their talents are equal to or greater than those required to be a good teacher, still, the effort, contribution, and talent cannot be so much more valuable as to justify the vast discrepancy between the salary of teachers and the salary of baseball players. It is hard to see how anyone could argue that Kirby Puckett *deserves* to earn in one year twice the amount that Mrs. Cottle will earn in forty years. No conceivable criterion that makes rewards proportional to desert could yield such a result.

Yet, these salary differences are the result of the working of market forces of supply and demand, and they are regarded as legitimate within a capitalist system. From an institutional point of view, they are legitimate, and baseball players are "entitled" to what they get. Likewise, teachers are entitled to what they get and no more. What this shows, however, is that what people are entitled to in a system that allocates in accord with market value is not the same as what they would receive in a system that allocates in accord with what people deserve.

What does determine what people morally deserve? In discussing this example, I mentioned three things that are often taken to determine what people deserve: their effort (how hard they work), their achievement (the value of the results of their work), and their abilities (the level of skill that is required to do their work). I am not going to try to decide which of these provides the best measure of what people deserve. This is not necessary here because it is clear that the result of distributing resources in accord with any of them would be very different from the result produced by a market economy. The distribution of resources in a purely capitalist economy is determined in large part by factors that have nothing to do with what people deserve: supply and demand and inheritance.

SUPPLY AND DEMAND

To see that capitalism does not reward desert, imagine a situation in which a person works hard and produces something of value. Will that person be well rewarded according to his deserts in a capitalist system? He may be, but he may not be.

Whether people are well paid depends on many things that have nothing to do with them, their efforts, and the value of what they produce. If the supply of labor is low and there is a steady demand for it, individuals are likely to do well. But the labor supply depends on the size of the population and the opportunity for people to acquire skills. If the population increases and the number of people who acquire relevant skills goes up, then the same person, working as hard as ever and producing as much value as ever, will earn less. If the population decreases and fewer people have skills, he will earn more. Yet in both cases, he is doing the same thing and would appear to be equally deserving in each situation.

What we deserve seems to depend on facts about ourselves, but the forces that determine the market value of a person's work do not depend on such facts. Whether the population is large or small and whether the skills in question are common or uncommon have nothing to do with that person's individual activities and are entirely determined by things over which he has no control. So, while the wages of such a person will vary in these different circumstances, it is hard to believe that what he actually deserves varies, since we are supposing that his work remains the same throughout. As the nineteenth-century philosopher and economist Henry Sidgwick concluded: "It does not seem that any individual's social Desert can properly be lessened merely by the increased number or willingness of others rendering the same services."[4]

[4] Henry Sidgwick, *The Methods of Ethics*, 7th ed. (New York: Dover Books, 1966; originally published 1907), 288.

INHERITED ADVANTAGES

The right of owners to pass on their wealth to heirs after death is an important aspect of private property rights as they are understood in a capitalist system. The arguments for permitting this are straightforward. People should be able to do what they want with their own money, and if they care about their children or other people, they should be able to pass on wealth to them after their own deaths. As Milton Friedman has said, "it seems illogical to say that a man . . . may use his income for riotous living but may not give it to his heirs."[5]

In spite of its widespread acceptance as an obvious right, the right of inheritance is incompatible with reward according to desert in two important ways. First, the recipient may not deserve the resources received. There is nothing to prevent someone from bequeathing money to a person who is lazy and unproductive. Indeed, there is nothing to keep one from bequeathing money to people who are guilty of dreadful crimes. The recipient's right to money from an inheritance derives entirely from being chosen by the person making the bequest and is in no way connected to the recipient's deserving anything.

Second, when large inheritances are passed on to children within a family, this not only gives recipients undeserved goods; it also gives them competitive advantages over other people. Inheritances can be used to become educated, to acquire skills, and to make investments. They provide people with the capital to launch careers and businesses and thus make it more likely that their possessors will succeed in a competitive economy. They are more likely to succeed not because they deserve success but rather because less fortunate people lack assets and have a harder time positioning themselves to do well in a competitive market.

Inheritances create unequal opportunities for people, and, as a result, people who are equally willing to work and have equal native talents will not have the same chance to be equally productive. They will not have the same opportunity to become deserving of resources. If we assume, for example, that physicians deserve high pay (because they work hard and do much good for people), then whether a person can come to deserve the high pay that physicians earn will depend on whether she has the money to go to medical school. If there are two equally able people and one can go to medical school because she has inherited much money and the other cannot because she lacks an inheritance, then they do not have an equal chance to deserve a doctor's earnings.

One might think that these advantages are offset by the availability of public education, which is freely available to all and funded by taxation. While all advanced societies provide such education, it is important to see free education is a welfare good that would not be provided in a libertarian capitalist society. In a libertarian society, education would be available only to those who can purchase it or receive it as a gift. To distribute public edu-

[5] Friedman, *Capitalism and Freedom* (Chicago: University of Chicago Press, 1962), 164.

cation to all departs from the market ideal because it distributes a costly resource to people independently of whether they have the money to pay for it. While publicly funded education is compatible with the welfare state and with socialism, it is not compatible with libertarian capitalism. This would be true even if the government gave tuition vouchers to students rather than running schools.[6]

Even if there is public education, undeserved inheritances will still give some people significant advantages. They will do this, for example, by allowing people who inherit wealth to go to expensive schools that are better or more prestigious. When competitive advantages and disadvantages like these exist, it becomes less plausible to claim that those who are less productive are morally less deserving than those who are productive. We don't know how the less productive would have done if they had enjoyed a greater range of opportunities. Hence, the claim that people in a capitalist system deserve their unequal incomes is seriously weakened by facts about inheritance and its effects.

Of course, inheritance of money is not the only factor that produces these inequalities. Natural talents and abilities are distributed unequally as well, and family background plays an important role in people's acquiring the social, psychological, and cognitive skills that make success more or less likely. These familiar facts only reinforce my overall point. The larger the role that these sorts of factors play in determining whether people succeed, the less plausible is the claim that people are personally responsible for their own success and deserve whatever benefits their success brings with it.

MORAL DESERT AS A PATTERNED CONCEPTION OF JUSTICE

Earlier I noted Robert Nozick's useful distinction between "historical" and "end-state" criteria of justice. Nozick claims that what people have done to deserve their resources is a factor that end-state criteria (such as utilitarianism or socialist equality) fail to consider. Nozick claims that his own entitlement conception of justice does take account of how people acquire their resources, since it looks at whether the acquisition occurred through a voluntary process or not. For him, any distribution is just if it results from voluntary processes of exchange and gift giving.

In addition to contrasting the libertarian capitalist view with "end-state" theories, Nozick also contrasts it with what he calls "patterned" conceptions of justice, and he argues that all patterned conceptions of justice are mistaken. What is a patterned conception of justice? It is a conception that requires that the distribution of goods conform to a certain pattern in order to be just. So, for example, strict equality is a patterned conception because it requires that a distribution consist of equal shares for all. We can tell whether a distribution does so quite easily by looking at the amount that each person pos-

[6] For discussion of education from a libertarian perspective, see Jan Narveson, *The Libertarian Ideal* (Philadelphia: Temple University Press, 1988), 275–81; and Loren Lomasky, *Persons, Rights, and the Moral Community* (Oxford: Oxford University Press, 1987).

sesses. Consider again the comparison from the beginning of this chapter.

	Situation A	Situation B
Person 1	1000	250
Person 2	1000	250
Person 3	1000	3000

It is easy to see that A conforms to the pattern of equal distribution and that B fails to do so. If justice requires equality, then A is just and B is unjust. Utilitarianism is also a patterned theory, for it requires the distribution to conform to whatever arrangement produces the largest total amount of well-being. Using that pattern, B would be just and A unjust.

The principle of need is also a patterned conception, for it requires that the distribution of goods be proportional to people's needs. The greater a person's needs, the larger the share that is due to that person. In order to construct such a distribution, we would first need to rank people by the magnitude of their needs, and then we would distribute resources to people in accord with this magnitude. A needs-based pattern of distribution would look like this:

	Need	Resources
Person 1	1000	1000
Person 2	100	100
Person 3	10	10
Person 4	1	1

If distribution according to need is required by justice, then this distribution is just because it perfectly matches amounts of resources to the magnitude of people's needs.

Nozick argues that all patterned criteria of justice are mistaken. His basic argument (which I will discuss more fully later) is that the implementation of any patterned conception of justice would require continuous interference with people's liberty and is therefore inconsistent with a free society. The reason for this is clear. If we begin with an ideal pattern in place and then permit people to buy and sell, spend and receive, give gifts, and do whatever they want with their holdings, the pattern will be disrupted. If we want to maintain the pattern, the government must either prevent people from using their resources as they wish or it must continuously undo the effects of their actions by redistributing things. For example, in the Wilt Chamberlain case, it would have to take away what he has received and redistribute it.

The difficulty for Nozick, is that while some of his remarks suggest that what people deserve is a relevant criterion of justice, the desert criterion is a patterned conception of exactly the sort he rejects.

If we take the ideal of giving people what they deserve seriously, we would need to rank people according to their degree of desert and then distribute goods in proportion to how deserving they are. The most deserving people would get the most resources, less deserving people would get less resources, and negatively deserving people would be deprived of resources (through fines or imprisonment, for example). A desert-based distribution would look like this:

	Desert	Resources
Person 1	+1000	+5000
Person 2	+100	+500
Person 3	0	0
Person 4	-100	-500

This chart makes clear that the idea of rewards in accord with desert is a patterned conception of justice. Since Nozick (like every major advocate of libertarian capitalism) rejects all patterned conceptions, he must also reject distribution in accord with desert. The idea of rewarding people according to what they deserve is incompatible with the libertarian idea that any distribution is just if it arises from voluntary actions.

The upshot of this discussion is that people who take seriously the ideal of rewards in accord with desert will not find their ideal realized in a libertarian capitalist society.[7] This is so for two reasons. First, given the influence of both inheritance and supply and demand, there is no reason to believe that the process of distribution according to "market value plus gifts" does reward people in accord with what they deserve. Second, the criterion of justice that requires rewards in accord with desert is inconsistent with the principles of libertarian capitalism. Capitalism, as Nozick rightly argues, opposes all patterned conceptions of justice, and reward according to desert is just such a patterned conception.

This is not to deny that capitalism permits the deserving to be rewarded. In some cases, people who make significant efforts or contributions do succeed in the market, and we may feel that they deserve their larger share of resources. We should realize, however, that when this happens, it is a fortuitous result, something that may occur within a market system but which the market system is not designed to bring about.

SOCIALISM AND DESERT

Socialists should not be too quick to take delight in the conclusion that capitalism fails to live up to the ideal of rewarding the deserving. Before we draw any conclusions about the relative merits of capitalism and socialism, we need to see whether socialism does a better job of living up to this ideal.

[7] For a strenous defense of the incompatibility between a market economy and the rewarding of desert, see Hayek, *The Mirage of Social Justice*, Volume 2 of *Law, Legislation, and Liberty*, (London: Routledge and Kegan Paul, 1976), chap. 9.

The place of desert in socialist thinking is somewhat complicated. Some of socialism's attraction seems to derive from an implicit appeal to the idea of personal desert. When socialists criticize capitalism because investors reap profits while workers gain little, they seem to be appealing to effort and contribution as criteria of desert. This idea is expressed in the following verse from a labor protest song.

> We worked to build this country, mister,
> While you enjoyed a life of ease.
> You've stolen all that we built, mister.
> Now our children starve and freeze.[8]

The song suggests that because workers put out the actual effort to produce things, it is they who deserve the rewards of their work. In contrast, owners and investors do not actually produce anything and, therefore, do not deserve the wealth that a capitalist system allows them to claim. Those who live a "life of ease" do not deserve to possess what has been built, while the workers deserve at least enough to provide for their children.

While socialism does appeal to the idea that people deserve to be paid in accord with their labor, this idea actually conflicts with socialism's commitment to equality and to distribution according to need. If distribution in proportion to work and contribution were implemented, the result would be a meritocracy of the productive and the diligent. If people varied widely in their efforts and contributions, this would lead to significant inequality, with highly productive people possessing much more than less productive or unproductive people. This result seems quite different from the socialist vision.

A socialist could reply that there is no conflict between rewarding the deserving and the ideal of equality because the differences between people's individual contributions are not so great as to merit large differences in people's possessions. If A deserves more because her efforts or contributions are larger than B's, that might justify some greater reward to A, but it would not justify a distribution that makes A exceedingly wealthy while leaving B in abject poverty. Samuel Bowles and Herbert Gintis, writing from a position that is sympathetic with socialist ideals, concede that good work should be specially rewarded. But, they say,

> the stakes should not be so high [as they are in contemporary capitalist societies] and . . . the penalties ought not to include deprivation of an acceptable living standard.[9]

In response to this claim, someone might object that people who make significant contributions deserve large rewards and that it would be wrong to limit inequalities to the modest level that Bowles and Gintis favor. In reply to this objection, socialists could appeal to a point made by Joel Feinberg, who notes that

[8] Jim Garland, "I don't want your millions, mister." In Alan Lomax, *Folk Songs of North America* (New York: Doubleday, 1960), 293.

[9] S. Bowles and H. Gintis, *Democracy and Capitalism* (New York: Basic Books, 1987), 207.

> *any* individual contribution will be very small relative to the immeasurably great contribution made by political, social, fortuitous, natural, and "inherited" factors. In particular, strict application of the "return of contribution" principle would tend to support a larger claim for the *community* to its own "due return," through taxation and other devices.[10]

Feinberg thinks that if we put the achievements of individuals in perspective, the claim that any single person has made huge contributions and thus deserves huge rewards will look implausible. Every individual accomplishment presupposes a reservoir of social and cultural resources, without which the individual achievements could not occur. Feinberg's claim is very plausible. If he is correct, then rewards for personal desert can be compatible with socialism because no one deserves the large-scale rewards that produce large disparities in resources among people. While some people might deserve more than others, the amount they deserve would not be so large as to produce a class society.

THE REJECTION OF THE PERSONAL DESERT CRITERION

While some socialists' arguments appeal to the connection between hard work and personal desert, in its purer forms, socialism appears to be committed to rejecting personal desert as a major factor in the distribution of resources. This comes out most clearly in the famous socialist slogan, "from each according to his ability, to each according to his needs." This two-part criterion appears to sever any link between a person's efforts and/or contributions and the resources that person should receive. According to this ideal, each individual is to make a contribution that is proportional to ability. At the same time, the amount that each individual receives should not depend on that person's output. Instead, it is based on another criterion entirely: the criterion of need. What people receive should be based on what they need and not on what they contribute.

Moreover, if the need criterion is met, then the criterion of equality is also satisfied. For if everyone's needs are met, then all are treated equally well, even if the satisfaction of different people's needs requires different resources or different amounts of the same resources. If A needs 1200 calories a day and B needs 2000, then we treat them equally well by giving them different amounts of food. If someone criticized this as a violation of the ideal of equality, insisting that equality requires us to give A and B the same amount of food, the socialist might reply that the objection simply shows that the critic has too rigid and simple a view of equality.[11]

[10] Feinberg, *Social Philosophy* (Englewood Cliffs, N.J.: Prentice Hall, 1973), 116. Feinberg credits this idea to L. T. Hobhouse, *The Elements of Social Justice* (London: Allen and Unwin, 1922), 161–63.

[11] For an analysis that stresses the varied and conflicting sense of equality see Douglas Rae, with Douglas Yates, Jennifer Hochschild, Joseph Monroe, and Carol Fessler., *Equalities*. (Cambridge, Mass.: Harvard University Press, 1981)

The key point here, however, is that anyone committed to distribution according to need must reject distribution according to personal desert, since what people deserve by virtue of their work and what they need are two different things. For this reason, socialists must reject personal desert as a criterion of justice.

It does not follow from this, however, that socialists entirely reject the ideal of giving people what they deserve. Instead, we can interpret them as operating with a different conception of desert. They focus on what I earlier called "human" desert. They believe that people deserve certain kinds of treatment simply by virtue of their being human and independent of their efforts, contributions, and abilities. They deserve, we might say, humane treatment, and humane treatment requires attention to their needs.

We can relate this ideal to the Kantian principle of treating people as ends in themselves and not as means only. If we take seriously the idea that each person possesses a value that is independent of his usefulness to other people, then the value of a person requires others to take his needs seriously . This is something that people deserve, whatever contribution they make or fail to make to others.

From the perspective of socialism, then, the most relevant form of desert is not individual or personal. Rather, it is *impersonal* or *human* desert. This is the form of desert that best fits in with the belief that all people deserve a fair share of their society's resources. To believe in *human* desert is to believe that some forms of treatment are due to people simply by virtue of their humanity. We can deserve these forms of treatment without doing anything to earn them. Socialists think that all people deserve a roughly equal share of the common good or an amount proportional to their needs, irrespective of what they personally have done.

DOES SOCIALISM GIVE PEOPLE WHAT THEY DESERVE?

Having examined the attitudes of socialists toward the ideal of giving people what they deserve, we need to evaluate socialism from the perspective of people who care about giving people what they deserve. Does socialism meet this criterion?

The answer here is mixed because, as we have seen, there are two different concepts of desert—personal desert and human desert. If we favor rewarding personal desert (based on effort or achievement) in a way that will lead to significant inequalities, then socialism will not be acceptable since it forbids such inequalities. In a socialist society, those who contribute much and those who contribute little will have roughly equal shares of the communal product. Many people disapprove of this result. They are morally offended by the idea that hard-working, productive people get no more than lazy, unproductive people. They believe this to be unjust, and their view has some plausibility.

This criticism of socialism must be tempered, however, with the recognition that capitalism is also deficient from this perspective. It permits many hard-working people to earn much less than people who work less hard or do not work at all. By permitting inheritances, it allows substantial resources to be transferred without any regard to work or merit at all. The failure of socialism to reward personal desert, then, does not constitute an argument for capitalism, since it too fails to make rewards proportionate to the value of people's work.

Capitalism's failure here, however, is different from socialism's. Socialism rejects the legitimacy of these differential rewards and seeks to produce a society in which they would not exist. In contrast, capitalism permits rewards based on desert but does nothing to guarantee that this will occur. In a capitalist society, many deserving people will not do well, but some people who work hard will succeed by virtue of their efforts and accomplishments. So, in individual cases, the ideal of rewards in accord with personal desert may be satisfied, even though the principle only plays a very small role in determining the overall shape of the distribution of goods.[12]

If we evaluate socialism from the perspective of "human" desert, the result is quite different. Socialism succeeds in giving people what they deserve simply by virtue of their being human beings. Pure capitalism, on the other hand, does not guarantee that any of a person's needs will be met. If there is such a thing as human desert, then, and if people deserve either an equal share of the social wealth or even just enough to meet their basic needs, this is something that socialism aims to provide. Libertarian capitalism rejects this ideal entirely. Libertarians must either reject the notion of human desert entirely or claim that the only thing that people humanly deserve is the ability to engage in voluntary activities (that do not violate others' rights) without the interference of others.

THE WELFARE STATE SOLUTION

Suppose that we accept the idea that desert should play some role in distribution and that we are sympathetic both to the idea of personal desert and the idea of human desert. From this perspective, we are likely to be unhappy with both capitalism and socialism. We will be unhappy with capitalism, first, because the rewarding of personal desert plays too small a role in a capitalist economy and, second, because nothing is guaranteed to people on the basis of human desert. We will be unhappy with socialism because of its failure to give enough recognition to personal desert as relevant in the distribution of goods.

One response to this situation is to construct a hybrid view that rejects the features of capitalism and socialism that fail to give desert its due, while accepting the features that succeed in giving desert its due. Proponents of the welfare state can claim that their view does precisely this. For the welfare state ideal gives personal desert the same role that it has in a capitalist system while at the same time recognizing the human desert that socialists empha-

[12] For an interesting discussion of the factors that influence the distribution of rewards in different professions, see Bok, *The Cost of Talent*. (New York: The Free Press, 1993).

size. The following chart makes clear how the welfare state combines the positive features of the other systems while avoiding their negative features.

	Personal Desert	**Human Desert**
Capitalism	Some role	No
Socialism	No	Yes
Welfare State	Some role	Some role

The welfare state solution looks attractive because it permits personal desert to operate as a factor in the distributive system, but it does not neglect human desert. It allows people to get ahead by virtue of their efforts, while recognizing that people who do not succeed in the market have a legitimate claim to at least some essential resources.

Recall that a welfare state system is one in which resources are distributed according to market value, supplemented by gifts and by some level of legally guaranteed publicly funded distribution of resources. Because the market system still operates in a welfare state, people can earn more than others through market success. In those cases where this success results from people's superior efforts and contributions, it will give them the rewards they deserve.

While the welfare state permits some reward in accord with desert, its underlying logic incorporates a skepticism toward the view that all holdings are deserved. It recognizes that the level of economic resources that people possess depends on many factors that have nothing to do with desert. For this reason, taxation to support a "safety net" or other forms of public distribution of resources is not an injustice because taxing people's holdings does not take away what they deserve. Much of what people possess is undeserved—either because it came to them through processes (such as inheritance) that have nothing to do with effort or contribution, or because, even where their efforts were required, they do not deserve the specific amount of holdings that they have acquired through the market system. To return to our baseball example, a good player may deserve a high salary, but he does not deserve a salary that is one hundred times larger than that of a school teacher. Nor do current players deserve more than the great players of the past. They are just lucky to be living in an era in which television advertising makes high salaries for players economically viable.

Taxation, then, does not usually deprive people of their just deserts because most of what they possess is not justly deserved. Even where people do deserve some amount of recompense, there is no rule that says that they deserve some precise amount of dollars. At most, they could be said to deserve something vague, such as a high standard of living.

In any case, as we have already seen, defenders of capitalism need to be careful in their appeals to desert. If we took the criterion of desert seriously and tried to implement it, this would have quite radical consequences. Inheritances would be abolished, since they constitute unearned wealth. Windfall profits (for example, money from an oil well that is discovered on your property) would be ruled out, since they are not based on any activities that merit them. Finally, money from investments might not qualify as deserved.

I am not arguing that we should make these changes. Rather, I am trying to show how much a capitalist economy departs from the standard of reward in accord with personal desert. Welfare state defenders can use this point to argue for the legitimacy of taxation to support welfare state activities. They have a ready reply to critics who complain that taxation for welfare state activities deprives taxpayers of money they justly deserve. In most cases, this is simply false.

What these reflections show is that both capitalism and socialism fail to capture all that a commitment to rewarding desert would imply. The welfare state does a better job of recognizing both aspects of the ideal of desert. While it does not perfectly realize the ideal of rewards in proportion to desert, it comes closer to that ideal than either of its competitors.

IS THE PERSONAL DESERT CRITERION ADEQUATE?

If what I have said is correct, then neither capitalism, socialism, nor the welfare state perfectly matches the distribution we would get by making rewards proportionate to moral desert. What should we conclude from this disparity between what people deserve and what these systems provide? Does it show that none of these systems is just? Does it show that we should substitute a desert-based system of rewards for a market economy, a socialist economy, or a welfare state?

I think it would be a mistake to try to introduce a distribution based on personal desert. There are three reasons for this.

First, even if people don't personally deserve the rewards they can acquire in a welfare capitalist system, it may still be beneficial to the economy to permit these rewards to function as incentives. If there is a scarcity of a particular skill, it may be worth paying more to people who have that skill, even though they don't deserve their natural talents or the advantages that permitted them to develop their skills.

Second, even if we can judge that some people earn more or less than they deserve, that does not mean that the criterion of desert can provide us with a precise scale for determining income. How could we rank teachers versus doctors, for example, in such a scale? Where would farmers or truck drivers fit in? What about people who work in nursing homes or supermarkets? What do artists and musicians deserve? When we start thinking about creating a ranking, whether we base it on effort or on the value of contribution, it is not clear how to proceed.

Third, as F. A. Hayek has argued, if we were to construct and implement such a desert scale, this would grant government agencies a dangerous power, the power to evaluate the worth of people and their activities. This would institutionalize a coercive power that could favor conventionalism and discourage innovation. It would impose a hierarchy of values that is incompatible with a pluralist society that is committed to letting people explore many different options and activities.[13]

In short, it is not clear that implementing a desert-based distribution scale is either possible or desirable. This is not to say that judgments about what people deserve are impossible, but making them the centerpiece of a system of distribution would be both difficult and dangerous.

What follows from this rather skeptical conclusion? There are two points of importance. First, arguments that capitalism is just because it rewards hard work and achievement or because it gives people what they deserve are not plausible. Socialists have been correct to attack the desert claims often made in defense of capitalism. Indeed, as I noted earlier, capitalism's most sophisticated defenders (thinkers such as Milton Friedman, F. A. Hayek, and Robert Nozick) do not try to justify it on this ground (though some of Nozick's remarks give the impression that he does).

Second, as we saw, because it is difficult to determine precisely what a person deserves, one argument against taxation to support welfare state activities is seriously weakened. One cannot plausibly argue that the welfare state unjustifiably deprives people of the just deserts of their work when it takes a portion of their earnings in taxes. This claim is weakened because even if a person deserves something, he does not deserve some precise dollar amount (such as the equivalent of his take-home pay). Moreover, since it is unclear that people deserve what they acquire in the market at all, taxation need not take from them what they do deserve.

As we saw in the last chapter, taking some portion of people's earnings need not destroy their incentive to work. So likewise, taking some portion of earnings in taxes need not violate their right to keep what they justly deserve. In neither case are we dealing with an all or nothing phenomenon. The justice of a tax depends in part on what it is for and on how much is taken. There is no reason to accept arguments against the welfare state based on the demand that people be allowed to keep all their earnings because they deserve them.

SUMMING UP

Many people would like to see a world in which people get what they deserve. While none of the systems I have considered lives up to this standard, the standard by itself does not provide a realistic, adequate guide to distribution. A welfare state system meets it partially by allowing (though not guaranteeing) some larger rewards that derive from personal effort and contribution. It also provides some resources to people outside of the market system and thus recognizes the sort of human desert that socialists emphasize. While it fails to meet the desert criterion fully, it comes closer to meeting it than pure forms of either capitalism or socialism.

[13] Hayek, *Mirage of Social Justice,* 69, 109.

CHAPTER SEVEN

Protecting Liberty

Advocates of both capitalism and socialism claim to prize freedom, and both claim that their favored system best protects and promotes liberty. This is not surprising because most of us value liberty and believe that in a just society, people will be relatively free to do what they want.

There are some actions, of course, that we do not think people should be free to do: acts of unprovoked violence against others, for example, or other acts that harm people or violate their rights. But once we exclude these illegitimate acts, we tend to think it is desirable to let people live according to their own choices. Few of us would choose to live in a society that severely limits our freedom. We want the right to do what we think is best, and consistency seems to require that we favor the same degree of liberty for others.

Since we value our liberty and since each side claims to protect it best, we need to decide who has the better case. In addition, we need to see how both these systems compare with the welfare state as guarantors of freedom.

CAPITALIST VERSUS SOCIALIST FREEDOM

One difficulty in settling the dispute between capitalists and socialists about freedom is that each has a different conception of freedom. Because of this, they disagree not only about how to evaluate particular situations but also about how to describe them. What one counts as a gain in freedom the other sees as no gain at all.

In order to understand this difference, consider an ideal libertarian capitalist society. Everything that people possess is acquired either directly from nature and or through voluntary transfers between people. No one is forced to engage in any transfers, and no one is prevented from doing so. People are perfectly free to buy and sell goods or to give them away. What people have is a result of market processes, gifts, and acquisitions of things from nature.

At the same time, some people have little or no goods. They do not succeed in the market and receive little or nothing as gifts, charity, or inheritance. They cannot eat properly, clothe themselves, or find suitable shelter. Though not directly prevented from doing what they want by any specific persons or group, they frequently find themselves unable to do what they want.

Socialists claim that in such a society, many people are not free. Because they lack the resources that are necessary for many activities, they cannot do many things that are necessary for a decent life. According to defenders of capitalism, however, these unfortunate people *are* free to do what they like because no one is preventing them from doing so. To be free, for libertarians, is to be free from interference or coercion by other people. Freedom, they say, must be distinguished from ability. According to the capitalist criterion, everyone in this society is free because no one is preventing them from doing what they want. Socialists, however, take the opposite view, arguing that people without resources are not free because they lack the ability to act in accord with their needs and desires.

There are two different conceptions of freedom, then. Capitalists think in terms of *negative* freedom, the freedom *from* interference by other people, while socialists emphasize *positive* freedom, the actual *ability to do* things that we want to do.[1]

The contrast between the two can be further sharpened by considering an ideal socialist society. In this society, resources are distributed equally according to need. All people are free in the sense that they are equally able to satisfy their needs. On the other hand, if activities like trade, gift giving, and investment would lead to inequalities, these activities would be forbidden or restricted. The government would prohibit these transactions or levy taxes that would alter the distribution that results from them.

Would people be free in this society? Would there be more or less freedom than in a capitalist society? From the libertarian capitalist perspective, this situation is a nightmare. Because they define freedom as freedom from interference rather than in terms of ability to act, libertarians would see this situation as one of all loss and no gain. Previously permitted actions would now be forbidden by governments, thus diminishing liberty, while the increased ability to act that would be enjoyed by many people would not be counted as a gain in liberty at all.

Socialists would say that there is a significant increase in liberty, since they would count the ability of people to act so as to satisfy their needs as an increase in freedom. While socialists could acknowledge that the prohibition

[1] For debates about understanding the nature of liberty, see David Miller, ed., *Liberty* (Oxford: Oxford University Press, 1991).

of trading activities limits the freedom of some, they would see this as the necessary price to pay in order to ensure the most extensive distribution of fundamental freedoms to all.

Which view of freedom is more reasonable? Should we understand freedom negatively as the absence of human interference? Or should we see it positively as the ability to act?

I believe that socialists have the better case in this debate about how to define freedom. Because they define freedom as ability, they can acknowledge that there is some loss of liberty in the transition from capitalism to socialism. They can acknowledge that when the government prevents people from engaging in activities, it does diminish their ability to act. Interference by government or other individuals is one of the sources of "unfreedom." So, while socialists believe that, on balance, liberty is increased by guaranteeing that people can meet basic needs, they need not deny that some liberty is lost in the process.

By contrast, the libertarian capitalist conception of liberty is too narrow. It seems unduly rigid to deny that anyone gains in liberty through socialism. The conception of freedom as the absence of interference by other people seems to rest on an arbitrary narrowing of the concept. If we think of freedom in this narrow way, it is hard to see why we consider it to be so valuable. Of course, we do not want others to prevent us from acting as we wish, but that is because we want to be able to act as we wish. We dislike *anything* that gets in the way of our acting freely; we don't limit our dislike just to active interference by other people. We value freedom because we value acting as we want to act. There is no reason to think that the only freedom we care about is freedom from interference by other people.

This is not to say that defenders of capitalism are wrong to care about negative liberty. Being prevented from acting by other people is a very important kind of constraint, and we will generally regard this kind of interference as an evil.

Nonetheless, it is arbitrary to think that we do or should care only about interference by other people. We also care about being prevented from doing what we want by natural events and situations. My freedom to travel along a particular road may be equally thwarted either by the presence of highway robbers or by floods and fallen trees. Both interfere with my liberty to go from one place to another. It would be irrational for me to care a great deal about being thwarted by thieves and not to care at all about being thwarted by water and trees. Both can constitute threats to my liberty to get where I want to go.

Socialists, then, are right to stress the importance of positive freedom, freedom as ability to act. Their concept is inclusive enough to recognize the value of negative freedom because human interference is one way in which our ability to act is diminished. At the same time, by stressing positive freedom, they recognize the importance of factors that are ignored and excluded by the libertarian capitalists' too narrow conception of freedom.

SOCIALISM AS A THREAT TO FREEDOM

While socialists are right about the importance of positive freedom, it does not follow that socialism actually protects positive freedom better than capitalism. It might turn out that socialist governments are not only a threat to negative freedom but a threat to positive freedom as well. In that case, socialism in practice would conflict not only with capitalist ideals but with socialist ideals of freedom as well.

The view that socialism is a threat to freedom can be defended both theoretically and historically. As a matter of theory, we can see that any government that is powerful enough to control the production and distribution of goods will also be powerful enough to act tyrannically toward its people. Since everyone would be dependent on this government for employment and for goods, it would hold a great deal of power over all citizens. By contrast, in a capitalist society, there are many possible employers and many possible sources of charitable help. There is not the high degree of centralized power that seems necessary for socialism to work. So, even if we accept the socialist idea that positive freedom is important, it may turn out that capitalism is more conducive to a free society because it permits greater diffusion of power and makes citizen less vulnerable to coercion by the government.

Going beyond theory, the history of the Soviet Union provides a bleak picture of what governments that are theoretically committed to socialist goals can turn out to be like in practice. The Soviet regime turned out to be a powerful source of interference with human freedom; at the same time it failed to provide sufficient material well-being to make positive freedom possible. In the words of Irving Kristol, a defender of capitalism,

> All that the various "socialist" societies have to show for the sacrifices they have demanded of their citizens is tyranny and scarcity.[2]

Kristol draws the following conclusion about the relative merits of capitalism and socialism.

> [T]hough capitalism may not be a sufficient condition for a liberal society, it does seem to be a necessary condition of it. History does not provide us with any instance of a society that repressed the economic liberties of the individual while being solicitous of his other liberties. It is the diffusion of wealth and power and status in a market economy that creates the "social space" within which civil and political liberty can flower, or at least be preserved to some degree.[3]

Kristol's claim, then, is that while not every capitalist society must be free, every free society must be capitalist.

Many people believe that history shows capitalism to be necessary for freedom and that socialist regimes are inevitably tyrannical. This historical

[2] Irving Kristol, *Two Cheers for Capitalism* (New York: New American Library, 1979), xiii.

[3] Ibid., xi.

argument is not without power, but it can never be a genuine proof. The tyrannical nature of the Soviet government was surely due in part to its roots in Czarist despotism and to the lack of democratic traditions in Russia. Socialists could claim that a history of failed versions of socialism does not prove that a better version of socialism could not work. As Andrew Levine, one defender of socialism, notes:

> Defenders of socialism today find themselves in something like the situation pro-capitalists might, if the only existing capitalist societies were, say, Botha's South Africa, Pinochet's Chile, or Hitler's Germany. . . . The fact that, to date, despotic social and political arrangements have been nearly universal under socialism . . . is not an insurmountable obstacle in the way of defending socialism. . . . [4]

From a purely logical point of view, Levine is clearly right. A string of socialist failures no more proves that socialism cannot succeed than the failure of pre-Wright brothers attempts at flying shows that airplanes are impossible.

Nonetheless, it would be foolish to ignore the historical record. Defenders of capitalism have warned that socialism would lead to tyranny, and history shows that this is not an idle worry. Perhaps socialism is possible, but trying to implement it has its dangers—the danger that it will fail to yield the goods promised and the danger that the attempt to create a socialist society will stifle freedom.

At the same time that we acknowledge the ways that a socialist state can threaten liberty, it is important to see that liberty can also be threatened in a capitalist state. Governments are not the only threat to liberty. If individuals or groups (such as corporations) acquire much greater material resources than others, they can use their resources to acquire a disproportionate share of power over others. One form of this power is political.

If we accept democratic political ideals, then we are committed to the view that all citizens should have roughly equal amounts of political influence. That is why we do not permit individuals to have more than one vote. It is also why congressional districts must be roughly equal in population.

Large accumulations of money, however, lead to vastly unequal amounts of political power. When individuals can use personal resources to run for office or to publicize their own views or to hire lobbyists, they acquire more political liberty than citizens who lack the resources to promote their views effectively. When candidates for public office have to rely on private contributions to pay for expensive campaigns, then they must pay special attention to the desires and interests of their political donors. In these ways, the value of the formal political rights that other citizens possess is much diminished.

Even if no wealthy individual, corporation, or group in a capitalist society is as powerful as the state is in a socialist state, such groups can amass power that directly limits the political liberty of less-well off citizens. As a result, wealthier citizens can use their influence to pass laws that advance their

[4] Andrew Levine, *Arguing for Socialism*, rev. ed. (London: Verso, 1988), 8–9.

interests at the expense of others, thereby diminishing both the well-being and the positive liberty of other citizens.

So, while we should accept the argument that socialist states can pose a serious threat to liberty, we should not overlook the threats to personal and political liberty that exist in capitalist states as well.

THE WELFARE STATE SOLUTION

If our goal is to enhance people's freedom by guaranteeing some of the resources necessary for acting to fulfill their aims, we may be able to achieve this without adopting the full socialist program. A democratic welfare state may combine the virtues of capitalism and socialism without acquiring their respective vices.

By guaranteeing every citizen some share of the resources needed for a decent life, the welfare state goes beyond the negative freedom of libertarian capitalism and toward the positive freedom stressed by socialists. It says that the market is not sufficient as a mechanism to provide all citizens with the resources that make positive freedom possible, and it uses the power of the state to ensure that all citizens have these resources.

At the same time, by leaving the market intact and allowing economic institutions to be independent of the government, the welfare state is less likely to give rise to a despotic, authoritarian government that stifles the free activity of its citizens. Since the welfare state leaves the market and the system of private ownership intact, it does not create the threat to freedom that is inherent in a government that controls all economic activity.

Threats to freedom are further diminished if the welfare state is a democratic government that recognizes rights of political participation and individual civil liberties. These institutional features of a government make it less likely that it can function tyrannically over its citizens.

From the perspective of enhancing freedom, then, a democratic welfare state is extremely attractive. It recognizes the importance of positive freedom and provides resources to enable citizens to act. At the same time, it recognizes the importance of negative freedom and the threats to freedom that powerful governments can create. It diminishes these threats by retaining the diffusion of social power that a market system can help to maintain, while at the same time adding rights of political activity and civil liberties to constrain government power.

To put the point succinctly, the welfare state provides some of the benefits of enhanced liberty that socialism aims for, while avoiding some of the threats to liberty that a full-fledged socialist government may bring with it. It retains some of the guarantees of negative liberty that defenders of capitalism stress, while taking steps to enhance positive liberty for all in a way that a pure market system cannot.

How is it that the welfare state is supposed to enhance liberty? Basically, it does this in the same way that it enhances well-being. In a pure capitalist society, those with abundant resources have a great deal of liberty because they have the resources that are necessary to pursue many of their goals. At the same time, people with meager resources do not have the ability to meet their basic needs or to pursue many of the things they want. By taxing those who are well off and transferring resources to those who are badly off, the welfare state enhances the liberty of badly off citizens substantially while interfering only minimally with the liberty of well-off citizens.

We can understand this point in terms of marginal utility, just as we did in talking about well-being. The marginal value of the freedom that well-off people possess diminishes with greater resources. The freedom to buy a third yacht is less valuable than the freedom to buy food and shelter for oneself and one's family. The amount by which taxation diminishes the freedom of the well off is smaller than the amount by which it enhances the freedom of the poor. The ability to meet one's needs enhances people's overall capacities much more than does the ability to purchase various kinds of luxuries. For this reason, even though a welfare state does limit the liberty of the well off, on balance, it creates much more freedom than a pure market society.

NOZICK'S CHALLENGE TO THE WELFARE STATE

While I have argued that the welfare state combines some of the virtues of capitalism and socialism while avoiding their vices, the legitimacy of the welfare state has been strongly challenged by Robert Nozick. Nozick attempts to show that any effort by governments to determine how resources are distributed will require illegitimate infringements of liberty. It is time to look more closely at this influential defense of libertarian capitalism.

Nozick has two main arguments to show that libertarian capitalism is the only system compatible with liberty and justice. The first argument centers on the idea that "liberty upsets patterns" and the second on the claim that "taxation is on a par with forced labor." The first argument is directed at a variety of theories of justice, including (but not limited to) egalitarian socialism and the welfare state. The second is more specifically directed against the welfare state and the idea that it is legitimate to tax some people in order to provide assistance or resources to others. I will consider each of these.

Nozick's first argument rests on two statements. First, every conception of justice except for the libertarian one requires that resources should be distributed in accord with some model or pattern. Second, the imposition of any of these patterns is incompatible with liberty.

One example of a patterned conception of justice is found in the socialist idea "to each according to their needs." According to this view, the amount of resources people should have is proportionate to their needs. The more they need, the more they should have; the less they need, the less they should have. If we adopt this ideal, we would decide whether a distribution in a society is just by seeing whether people with greater needs have greater resources than those with lesser needs. The distribution described in the chart below is just from this point of view because the right pattern exists in the relationship between need and resources.

	Degree of Need	Amount of Resources
Person A	+500	$500
Person B	+400	$400
Person C	+250	$250

If person A received less than person C, that would be unjust because it would not exhibit the right pattern.

Or, consider what is perhaps the simplest pattern, a strictly equal distribution of resources. If justice requires everyone to have the same amount of resources, it would be easy to tell whether a particular distribution is just. If everyone possesses the same amount, this would be just, and if they possess different amounts, it would be unjust. Equality, then, is a simple pattern insofar as it is easy to verify whether it is exhibited in a distribution or not.[5]

Other patterned conceptions would make resources proportional to other features. For example, someone who believes that teachers should earn more than baseball players or newspaper deliverers might construct a list of occupations, ranking them in terms of the contribution to social well-being that each type of work makes. According to this view, the desired pattern would require increasing (or decreasing) amounts of social contribution to be matched by increasing (or decreasing) amounts of money.

Much of our thinking about justice is influenced by beliefs about what kind of distributive pattern is required by justice, Nozick's "liberty upsets patterns" argument is an attempt to show that *every* patterned conception of justice is mistaken.

He argues as follows: Suppose that your favorite pattern were instituted. If you are an egalitarian, everyone would have the same amount of resources; if you believe in distribution in accord with social contribution or need or effort, then that distribution would be enacted. Let us call your favored distribution D1.

Now, returning to Nozick's Wilt Chamberlain example, suppose that after D1 is enacted, Wilt Chamberlain makes a deal to play basketball and to receive an extra 25 cents from every spectator. Because many people want to see him play, after a period of games, Chamberlain accumulates much more money than anyone else. Call this new distribution D2.

Is D2 a just distribution? From the point of view of the various patterned conceptions, we would have to answer no. Certainly, D2 is not an equal distribution. Nor does Chamberlain have greater needs than anyone else. Nor does he necessarily work hardest or make the greatest contribution to social well-being. Any of these patterned conceptions would condemn D2 as unjust.

[5] This example oversimplifies the demands of equality. For discussion of equality's complexities, see Douglas Rae et al., *Equalities* (Cambridge, Mass.: Harvard University Press, 1983).

Common sense suggests, however, that this new distribution is just. Nozick explains and justifies this common-sense reaction by appealing to the principle that "whatever arises from a just distribution by just steps is itself just."[6] If D1 was just and D2 came about by just steps, then D2 is just.

If D2 is just, however, then it is false that justice requires the pattern embodied in D1. D2 does not conform to any patterned conception of justice. Therefore, if D2 is just, every patterned conception of justice is mistaken.

Let us look carefully at this argument. It has three parts.

1. D1 is a just distribution.
2. D2 arises from D1 by just steps.
3. Therefore, D2 is a just distribution.

Is this argument sound?

Consider the first premise, the view that D1 is just. The argument is supposed to show that this is false, but this is not a charge that defenders of patterns will make. Remember that we assumed that each of us got to choose our favorite pattern. So no defender of D1 will object to this premise.

What about the steps by which D2 came about? Were they just? It is hard to see what is unjust about them. Many people freely choose to use their resources to see Wilt Chamberlain play basketball. It is hard to see how permitting them to pay extra to see him could constitute an injustice to them. So, if the initial distribution was just and the steps that redistributed people's resources were just, then the result was just, even though it no longer conforms to a pattern.[7]

What follows from this appears to be the conclusion that "liberty upsets patterns,"—if we permit people to act as they want, then no pattern can be maintained. On the other hand, if we want to maintain a pattern, we must deprive people of the right to use their resources as they wish. As a result, Nozick says, it is impossible to maintain any distributional pattern "without continuous interference in people's lives."[8]

DOES LIBERTY UPSET PATTERNS?

This is a powerful argument, and it certainly reveals difficulties with many plausible conceptions of justice. It is particularly powerful as an argument against a strictly egalitarian distribution, for it shows that if we want to maintain strict equality, we must give people resources (money, for example) and then prohibit them from using them. The only way to ensure that everyone has the same amount of money is to prevent people from spending their money to purchase things they want. So a pure egalitarian distribution of

[6] Nozick, *Anarchy, State and Utopia*, 151.

[7] For a more skeptical view of the justice of these transactions, see G.A. Cohen, "Robert Nozick and Wilt Chamberlain: How Patterns Preserve Liberty," in J. Arthur and W. Shaw, eds., *Justice and Economic Distribution*, 2nd ed. (Englewood Cliffs, N.J.: Prentice Hall, 1991), 214–19.

[8] Nozick, *Anarchy, State, and Utopia*, 163.

money would require total rigidity and severe, self-defeating limits on what people can do with their money. Clearly, this is absurd, and Nozick's argument makes this absurdity evident.

But is every pattern incompatible with liberty in this way? Has Nozick shown that the cost of implementing every conception of justice (other than his own) is "continuous interference with people's lives"? This conclusion does not follow. The reason it does not follow is that there are many possible kinds of patterns, and some patterns permit more flexibility than the ones we have so far considered.

Consider one pattern that is identified with certain conceptions of the welfare state. Suppose that one's criterion of justice is that no one should fall below a certain minimum amount of resources. According to this view, each citizen should be provided with enough resources to meet his or her basic needs. Apart from this one requirement, people may have whatever they acquire through the market, as gifts, or from charity.

If this pattern were enforced, Wilt Chamberlain could still make his arrangement, basketball fans could still pay extra to see him, he could still become very wealthy, and so on. There would be no continuous interference in people's lives. Money and other goods could be distributed in diverse ways, and the amounts held by different people could vary enormously and change constantly. Nonetheless, there would be a pattern, and we could tell whether a distribution conforms to the pattern by seeing whether anyone falls below the minimum required for a decent life. We could call this the "guaranteed minimum" conception of justice.

My point here is not to prove that this is the right conception of economic justice. Much needs to be considered in order to decide whether this conception is correct. This conception does have some important virtues, however.

First, it does not appear vulnerable to Nozick's objection that "liberty upsets patterns." People in a society that implemented a guaranteed minimum would still have a great deal of liberty. They could engage in all the transactions that are characteristic of a market economy, and through the market, different people could acquire varying amounts of money and other resources. Some could still be very wealthy.

Second, this conception, while a far cry from a pure egalitarian or needs based distribution, would meet some of the goals that socialists want to achieve. The direst poverty would no longer exist. People would not starve or freeze because of lack of resources. Everyone's most pressing needs, those associated with physical survival, would be met.

A welfare state that provided a basic minimum to all citizens, then, would leave intact most of what advocates of capitalism favor, while addressing people's most pressing needs and thus responding in part to a central concern of socialists. Socialists have always expressed outrage that capitalism permits some people to go hungry while others wallow in wealth and plenty. They could not make this criticism of a welfare state that guaranteed people a decent level of well-being.

Such a guaranteed minimum, then, is a pattern that has some attractive features. It is a conception of justice that is patterned and nonetheless permits a great deal of liberty. By combining these two properties, it shows that Nozick is mistaken in thinking that every patterned conception of justice is incompatible with a free society.

IS TAXATION ON A PAR WITH FORCED LABOR?

While the "guaranteed minimum" ideal would permit a great deal of liberty, libertarian opponents of the welfare state will still object to it. They can appeal to Nozick's second argument to support their view.

Even though a welfare state that provides a guaranteed minimum to all would not require continuous interference with people's liberty and would not prohibit the kinds of exchanges exemplified in the Wilt Chamberlain example, it would require taxation to finance this minimum. Taxation, however, is not a voluntary exchange. It is a coercive exchange. Citizens are required by law to contribute, and if they fail to do so, they may face confiscation of their resources, fines, or imprisonment. For these reasons, libertarians object to using taxation as a means of providing all citizens with a guaranteed minimum. They see such taxation as a significant interference with people's liberty. Nozick brings this idea out forcefully by claiming that taxation "is on a par with forced labor."[9]

How are taxation and forced labor supposed to be alike? They have three features in common. First, they are both *forced*. Neither is a voluntary activity. Second, just as forced labor involves working for the government, so, Nozick argues, if 20 percent of our income is paid in taxes, then we are in effect working for the government for 20 percent of our working hours. Finally, forced labor is wrong. It is a kind of slavery, and since taxation shares the first two properties with forced labor, it too is wrong. It violates the rights of the person being taxed.

This argument has a great deal of rhetorical appeal. People often resent taxes, and the argument seems to provide a theoretical account that both explains and justifies this resentment.

In the context of Nozick's book, however, the argument is deeply flawed. It is deeply flawed for a very simple reason. Nozick himself accepts the legitimacy of taxation. He believes that it is legitimate to tax people in order to support the police, the courts, the army, and the other institutions of the "minimal state." If he did not believe this, he would be an anarchist.

So, there is an inconsistency in Nozick's view that creates a serious problem for any defender of libertarian capitalism who is not an anarchist. Anarchists have a consistent view. They reject all forms of government coercion, including taxation, as illegitimate. Most people, however, think that at least some forms of government coercion (like preventing murder and assault) can be legitimate, and this requires that they accept some form of taxation. Taxation is nec-

[9] Ibid., 169.

essary because without it, government cannot carry out its legitimate tasks. Even a "minimal" or "night watchman" state must impose taxes on its citizens.

So, Nozick (like other libertarian defenders of the minimal state) must make one of two choices. Either he must retract the claim that taxation is on a par with forced labor. Or he must admit that forced labor is sometimes morally legitimate. Once the legitimacy of taxation for some purposes is accepted, there is no longer any principled basis for claiming that taxation to meet people's minimum needs is immoral while taxation to protect them from force and fraud is perfectly fine. It is arbitrary to object vehemently to taxation that guarantees every citizen protection from hunger and cold while accepting taxation that protects every citizen against attacks by other people.

Since Nozick and other libertarian capitalists accept some taxation, they need to show why welfare state activities are not legitimate. Suppose that they attempt to do so by appealing to the principle (stated by Nozick) that government "may not use its coercive apparatus for the purpose of getting some citizens to aid others."[10] If they appeal to this principle, then they must join the anarchists in rejecting taxation to pay for police protection for all people. This is because paying for police protection with tax money is an instance of using the coercive powers of government "for the purpose of getting some citizens to aid others."

Indeed, if we understand a welfare state as any state that provides resources to citizens independently of their ability to pay, then a libertarian capitalist "minimal state" *is* a kind of welfare state.[11] It distributes the good of police protection to all, whether or not they can pay for it, and it does this by taxing citizens who can pay. If well off citizens do not want to pay, they must, even if they would rather purchase private security protection for themselves.

If the so-called "minimal state" is itself a kind of welfare state, then what separates libertarian capitalists from welfare state defenders is not a matter of deep principle. Rather, it is a matter of judging how extensive the distribution of resources to citizens should be. Minimal state advocates think that very few goods should be distributed by the government, while welfare state advocates think a more generous distribution is necessary. Both, however, accept the legitimacy of taxation for the purpose of providing at least some goods to all.

WHERE DO WE STAND?

In this chapter, I have tried to show that the welfare state provides a better solution to the problem of liberty than either a libertarian capitalist order or a socialist system.

The welfare state recognizes the importance of positive liberty (the ability actually to do things) that socialists stress and tries to increase positive liberty by providing at least some resources to all citizens. At the same time, the

[10] Nozick, *Anarchy, State, and Utopia*, ix.

[11] Nozick seeks to show, unconvincingly I think, that the "minimal state" is not redistributive. For his argument, see *Anarchy, State, and Utopia*, 27, 113ff.

welfare state recognizes the importance of the negative liberty (freedom from interference by other people) that capitalists emphasize, and it takes seriously the worry that a socialist state would accumulate so much power that the government becomes a threat to people's liberty. So, the welfare state distributes some goods through the government while permitting private ownership and the market economy to exist, thus gaining the benefit of diffused social power.

In addition, as we saw, the welfare state avoids the excessive rigidity of many patterned conceptions of justice. It creates a distribution that is both patterned and compatible with liberty and thus avoids Nozick's arguments against patterned conceptions.[12]

Finally, although the welfare state uses taxation to support this distribution and although taxation is a coercive practice, advocates of the minimal state are in no position to criticize this since they accept the legitimacy of taxation for at least some government activities. Indeed, by distributing police protection to all, they unwittingly accept the basic principle of the welfare state—the principle that citizens should have access to at least some resources even if they cannot pay for them.

What this chapter and the preceding two show, then, is that if we evaluate capitalism, socialism, and the welfare state from the perspective of a concern for maximizing well-being, giving people what they deserve, and protecting liberty, the welfare state comes out best according to all three criteria. Cumulatively, this is a powerful argument for the legitimacy and desirability of the welfare state.

[12] For Nozick's own second thoughts about the libertarian view, see his *The Examined Life* (New York: Simon & Schuster, 1989), Chapter 25.

CHAPTER EIGHT

Rawls's Defense of the Liberal Democratic Welfare State

In this chapter, I will consider some of the central ideas developed by John Rawls in his book *A Theory of Justice*.[1] There are several reasons for discussing Rawls's views at this point. First, many people regard *A Theory of Justice* as the most important philosophical work on justice in this century. Second, because Rawls defends a form of welfare state, his theory can help us deepen our understanding of the moral basis for the welfare state. This is especially important because welfare state institutions have been subjected to much hostile criticism. If Rawls's theory can help expose the flaws in these criticisms, it will provide a valuable addition to my discussion.

Finally, by examining Rawls's theory, we can begin to approach the question of how extensive a welfare state is required by justice. Many different kinds of welfare state are possible. Some provide minimal resources to their citizens, while others are very generous. We need to know which type is required by justice. Only by determining this can we evaluate the economic systems of actual societies and decide which ones, if any, are just. We can look to Rawls's theory for guidance here, since it contains both a justification for a liberal democratic welfare state and a criterion for deciding how much a welfare state should provide to its citizens.

RAWLS'S METHOD

Rawls's justification for the welfare state has some distinctive features. In order to clarify them, it will be useful to contrast Rawls's method of argu-

[1] John Rawls, *A Theory of Justice* (Cambridge, Mass.: Harvard University Press, 1971). All page references are in the text.

ment with the method I have used in this book. I have proceeded by identifying the primary moral values that underlie major arguments for and against different economic systems: the promotion of well-being, the allocation of goods in accord with desert, and the protection of liberty. My argument proceeds by comparing each system's success in advancing these values. It is a cumulative argument, resting on several different values and a mixture of theoretical and practical considerations. While I have tried to argue carefully and systematically, there is a certain lack of unity in my approach, since it focuses on multiple factors that need to be weighed and balanced. Recognizing that many different factors and values are relevant, I try to wade through the plethora of relevant reasons, impose some order on them, and then, by evaluating the most central arguments, arrive at a conclusion.

Rawls employs a different, quite distinctive method of argument. While he sometimes considers familiar arguments and values, his basic method involves the construction of a single criterion for evaluating different conceptions of justice.

Rawls's criterion derives from the social contract tradition in political philosophy. He argues that the correct principles of justice are those that would be agreed to by people designing the basic institutions of their society. Instead of simply asking which principles of justice are true or which ones we appeal to in ordinary life, Rawls asks which principles we would choose if we were writing a social contract that contained the fundamental rules to govern our society.

Rawls's theory contains two main parts. The first part defends the social contract method and describes the conditions under which people make the choice of principles. The second part describes the principles of justice and defends them by showing why they would be chosen for inclusion in an ideal social contract.

THE ORIGINAL POSITION

If we ask what principles people would choose to govern their society, it may not be clear how this will help us find the correct principles of justice. After all, people disagree about what the principles of justice are and what kind of social, political, and economic system justice requires. If we simply ask what principles people would choose to govern their society, we will get many different answers rather than a single one.

In order to solve this problem, Rawls proposes that we describe the situation in which people choose principles in a special way that differs from actual circumstances. Rawls calls his theory "justice as fairness" because the situation in which the principles will be chosen must be fair. In addition, it must possess other features that make the principles credible.

To begin the search for the principles of justice, then, we are to imagine a group of people in what Rawls calls "the original position," a hypothetical situation in which no rules yet exist. Neither the people involved nor the situation are real. Both are idealized, and the first part of Rawls's thought experiment involves deciding what requirements to place on these people in order to ensure that the principles they would select are correct.

One restriction is that people in the original position must be regarded as having an equal voice and as agreeing freely to whatever principles they adopt. To see why these conditions of equality and uncoerced agreement are important, imagine a group that agrees to appoint George as the dictator of all and accepts the principle "do whatever George says." They select this principle because George has a powerful weapon and has threatened to kill everyone who opposes this rule. Because people accept this principle only under the threat of force, we would not take it seriously as a principle of justice. We will treat principles that emerge from the original position as correct only if they emerge from the free, uncoerced consent of equal parties. So, we are to imagine that the people in the original position are free and equal in this way.

A second condition is that people in the original position must be rational. The reason for this is obvious. If they are not rational, we will have no reason to take seriously the results of their deliberations. We must be assured that the principles are not the result of irrational acceptance.

Third, Rawls proposes that people in the original position must have a good understanding of human nature and human societies. The principles of justice are meant to provide a workable basis for social life. If their acceptance rests on false beliefs about individuals and social institutions, this will discredit them. The principles must be based on good information about human beings and human society.

A related point concerns the motivation of the people in the original position. Suppose that they are all extreme altruists and always put the interests of others first. While we might admire them for their virtue, we might also think that the rules that a group of saints would accept might not be suitable for normal people to live by. Normal people have a mixture of motivations. We may care about other people generally, but we tend to care most deeply about advancing our own interests and the interests of people who are near and dear to us.

To take account of these facts about human motivation, Rawls assumes that people in the original position are concerned with advancing their own interests. They want to make sure that their own lives will go well, and they want principles of justice that will protect them from various kinds of bad conditions.

In addition, Rawls supposes that these people are, as he says, "mutually disinterested." That is, when they deliberate about what principles to adopt, they do so from a perspective of concern for themselves and not for others. Each is trying to strike the best bargain for himself and does not worry about others. This does not mean that Rawls thinks that actual people are selfish or egotistical. Rather, he thinks that if we make the principles acceptable to people who care about themselves, then those principles will protect the basic interests of all. Again, we would not want principles that presuppose extreme altruism. The most credible principles are those that would be acceptable to "mutually disinterested" people who are concerned with advancing their own interests.

THE VEIL OF IGNORANCE

One of the most important conditions that Rawls places on the people in the original position is the "veil of ignorance." According to Rawls, the people in the original position must be ignorant of any particular facts about themselves. They cannot know who they are, what features they possess, or what specific position they will occupy in society. This may seem like a strange condition, but it is crucial to obtaining agreement on rules that are appropriate.

To see why the veil of ignorance is necessary, imagine that A and B are in the original position and are considering whether to adopt rules that permit slavery. If they know that A will be a master and B will be a slave and if they are concerned about pursuing their own advantage, then A will favor a system that permits slavery while B will reject this system. Agreement will be impossible, since both will simply reason in an unconstrained way about what will benefit them. We all recognize, however, that the claim "this will benefit me" or "this will harm me" is not an argument for the justice or injustice of an institution. The veil of ignorance is a means for disallowing such claims.

To see how it works, consider A and B again. If we place them behind the veil of ignorance, then neither knows whether he will be a slave or a master. Since neither one will want to be a slave and since neither one can know in advance what status he will have in a slave society, they must reject slavery altogether. In order to prevent themselves from being treated in an intolerable way, they must adopt principles that prohibit anyone from being treated that way. The only way to prevent the possibility of being a slave oneself is to adopt a principle that prohibits the institution of slavery. The veil of ignorance forces this choice, acting as an information shield that makes it impossible to adopt rules that advantage some at the expense of others.

This example highlights one of the key features of Rawls's view. There are certain conditions (such as being a slave) that any person would find intolerable. In order to protect oneself from being in that position, each person in the original position must insist on principles that guarantee no one should be in such a position. The resulting principles of justice prohibit forms of treatment that no one would want for themselves.

To summarize Rawls's method, then, he argues that the correct principles of justice are the ones that would be chosen by people who are free, equal, rational, knowledgeable about human nature and society, concerned about promoting their own well-being, mutually disinterested, and ignorant of their own identity and place in society. To say that a principle of justice is correct is to say that it would be chosen by people in this situation.

THE TWO PRINCIPLES OF JUSTICE

Rawls believes that people in the original position would choose two basic principles of justice, one for distributing basic political and civil liberties and one for distributing social and economic goods.

Here is the first principle:

> Each person is to have an equal right to the most extensive total system of equal basic liberties compatible with a similar system of liberty for all. (250)

The "basic liberties" that Rawls has in mind here are things such as freedom of speech and assembly, freedom of religion, freedom of political participation, and the protections of the "rule of law" (such as prohibition of arbitrary arrest, guarantees of due process of law). The liberties protected by the first principle are the familiar liberties of a liberal democratic state. They provide people with rights to influence the political process as citizens, and they create a system of immunities from interference by the government. In a just society, everyone will possess these liberties equally.

While these political and civil liberties may not seem related to issues of economic justice, the political and economic realms are interconnected in many ways. No state, Rawls thinks, can be just if it does not provide its citizens with these basic liberties. This is true even if it succeeds in making people economically prosperous. Rawls thinks that the political and civil liberties are so important that he gives them priority over economic rights. He does this by saying that his first principle has "lexical priority" over the second principle. The basic political and civil liberties come first; they may not be traded away or denied in order to promote economic progress.

Rawls's second principle concerns the distribution of social and economic goods. He develops it in two stages. In the first version, he writes:

> [S]ocial and economic inequalities are to be arranged so that they are both (a) reasonably expected to be to everyone's advantage, and (b) attached to positions and offices open to all. (60)

This principle expresses three important ideas. First, it tells us that justice permits "social and economic inequalities"; it does not require that everyone have the same amount of resources. Second, however, it requires that the overall system of distribution must be advantageous to all. Third, it insists that if higher rewards attach to some occupations, the opportunity to obtain those occupations must be open to all people.

As stated, this principle is not very definite about the nature of a just distribution of resources. Rawls considers several ways of making the principle more specific and finally settles on the one he calls "the difference principle." Its job is to tell us how much economic inequality is permitted by the principles of justice. The new version of the second principle contains two new features. It reads as follows:

> Social and economic inequalities are to be arranged so that they are both (a) to the greatest benefit of the least advantaged and (b) attached to offices and positions open to all under conditions of fair equality of opportunity. (83)

One change is contained in condition (b). It specifies that the greater rewards that attach to certain positions in society are just only if everyone has "fair equality of opportunity" to compete for those positions. The ideal of "fair equality of opportunity" requires that a just society provide some degree of education and training to everyone, independent of their ability to pay for it. If justice is to permit the greater rewards that go with some occupations, then the competition for those positions must be fair, and in order for the competition to be fair, people must have more than a legal right to apply for positions. They must also have some resources invested in the development of their skills so they can compete effectively. This is the moral basis for the view that government must provide everyone with a free education, at least up to a certain grade level.

THE DIFFERENCE PRINCIPLE

Many people think that if government provides free education for all, that is enough to create fair opportunities, and no further action is required to achieve economic justice. Rawls disagrees, and this is why he adds condition (a) to the second principle of justice. This condition, known as the "difference principle," says that economic inequalities are just only if their existence is "to the greatest benefit of the least advantaged." This means that economic inequalities can be just but only if they are part of a system that maximizes the well-being of those who possess least.

In order to make clear how the principle works, it will be useful to recall a comparison discussed in Chapter 4. Consider the following distributions of resources:

	Situation A	**Situation B**	**Situation C**
Person 1	1000	1250	1000
Person 2	1000	1250	1000
Person 3	1000	2000	2500

Situation A is a pure egalitarian distribution: Everyone has exactly the same amount. In situation B, one person has more than the others, but the others' holdings are increased too. If we assume that giving person 3 less than 2000 would result in less than 1250 for persons 1 and 2, then situation B satisfies the difference principle. Rawls would say that the move from A to B is just. By contrast, if we move to C, person 3 improves his holdings, but 1 and 2 are not brought up. Situation C is unjust according to the difference principle.

While this chart illustrates the key idea of the difference principle, there is one way in which it misrepresents Rawls's view. Rawls is concerned with what he calls the "basic structure" of society. He is not concerned with the amounts of resources that particular individuals possess. So, in making these comparisons, we should be thinking not about particular persons but rather about socioeconomic groups. The following chart better represents Rawls's concerns (although he does not identify these specific groups).

	Situation A	Situation B	Situation C
Unskilled worker	1000	1250	1000
Skilled worker	1000	1250	1000
Company Executive	1000	2000	2500

Rawls is concerned with the level of resources going to persons occupying particular social roles or statuses. That is what the basic principles of justice are about. They are a means of judging the basic structure of society and only apply secondarily to individuals.

Rawls's adoption of the difference principle shows that he accepts the idea that a system that permits inequalities may provide incentives that will result in benefits for all. Inequalities can be just if they have this positive effect.

In earlier chapters, this incentive argument came up as part of an argument for capitalism and the market system. As we saw, many people claim that greater rewards for some can lead to increased productive activity and thus to a greater pool of resources for increasing everyone's well-being. A major argument for market capitalism is that it has this effect. Its defenders claim that while some people acquire more resources than others, even those at the bottom are made better off by the general increase in social productivity.

By embracing this argument, Rawls seems to accept the logic of what is sometimes called "trickle down" economics. This is the view that greater benefits for wealthy people "trickle-down" to—and thus benefit—less well-off people.

Rawls's difference principle differs from "trickle-down" economics in a number of significant ways, however. First, it makes benefits for less well-off people a necessary condition of the justice of greater rewards for others. If the benefits for all that are said to arise from providing incentives do not actually occur, then Rawls requires that a purely egalitarian distribution be created. While most "trickle-down" theorists do not take equality seriously, Rawls sees it as the point to which we should return if increased rewards to some do not in fact benefit all.

Second, the expression "trickle down" suggests that the wealthy will have large amounts of resources while the amount that reaches people at lower levels will just be a trickle, a small amount. Rawls's difference principle, however, demands that inequalities be set up so as to maximize the well-being of people at the bottom of the economic ladder. This strongly suggests that a substantial amount of resources (not just a trickle) must find its way to poorer people if the holdings of the better off are to be justified.

Finally, since Rawls's theory requires that inequalities must maximize the well-being of the poor in order to be just, this suggests that every increase in inequality must be justified in terms of its improving the lot of the least well off. Only if it has this effect can an inequality be justified. For this reason, it might be more appropriate to call Rawls's view a "trickle-*up*" theory, since every movement of resources upward and away from equality must be justified by its tendency to promote the well-being of the least well off. Rather than simply hoping that the benefits of inequality will trickle down, Rawls's difference principle requires them to benefit the least well off. If they do not, then justice forbids them, and an equal distribution would be required.

DEFENDING THE DIFFERENCE PRINCIPLE

How does Rawls defend the difference principle? How does he show that it expresses the correct principle of justice regarding the distribution of social and economic goods?

Recall that for Rawls the best way to show that a principle of justice is correct is by showing that it would be adopted by people in the original position. This is precisely what Rawls tries to do for the difference principle. He tries to show why the difference principle would be adopted in the original position by people who are free, equal, rational, knowledgeable about human nature and society, concerned to promote their own well-being, mutually disinterested, and ignorant of their own identity and place in society.

The argument for accepting the difference principle has two parts because the principle itself has two parts. The first part states a presumption in favor of an equal distribution, while the second describes a condition under which an unequal distribution becomes permissible. So, in showing why the difference principle would be chosen, we need to know why people would choose equality as the starting point and then why they would be willing to move away from equality.

Why would they choose equality as a starting point? Each person is concerned with advancing his own interests and is not interested in advancing or diminishing the interests of others. That means that each one wants the best possible result for herself and does not have either an altruistic desire to make others better off or a hostile desire to make them worse off. So, each person will want as good a personal situation as possible.

In addition, because the terms of the contract must be acceptable to all, each person knows that an arrangement that makes some people better off than others will be rejected by those who do less well. At this stage, there is no reason to accept such inequalities. So, as a first step, the proposal of an equal distribution is the only one that would be agreed to by all.

Once we have gotten to this point, then the question is: Why would people ever agree to anything other than an equal distribution? The answer is that if an unequal distribution will make every person better off, then everyone would accept this—again because all are concerned with advancing their own interests.

Recall the choice discussed earlier.

	Situation A	Situation B
Unskilled worker	1000	1250
Skilled worker	1000	1250
Company executive	1000	2000

If we begin with the strict equality of situation A and can then show that allowing company executives to be better off will result in improving everyone's situation, then both the skilled and unskilled workers will find situation B preferable to situation A.

Now consider a different choice, a move from situation B to situation D.

	Situation B	**Situation D**
Unskilled worker	1250	800
Skilled worker	1250	1550
Company executive	2000	2500

By moving to situation D, two groups are made better off, but people in the lowest position are made less well off. This move would be condemned by the difference principle, since it creates inequalities that are not "to the greatest benefit of the least advantaged."

Would the move from B to D be rejected in the original position? Rawls argues that it would. Because the veil of ignorance prevents people from knowing what position they will occupy in society, everyone knows that they may end up in the lowest position. For that reason, they will want to ensure that the position of the least well off is as good as possible.

But, one might object, why wouldn't people in the original position be willing to gamble? If they permit inequalities like those in situation D and if they wind up in a better position, their gains will be larger. Maybe those larger gains are so good that they are worth the risk that one might lose and end up in the bad position.

Rawls rules out this gambling strategy, claiming that people in the original position would follow what is called a "maximin" strategy. They will aim not for the highest possible winnings but rather for a situation in which, even if they lose, their losing situation will be as good as possible. They will want to prevent finding themselves in an intolerable position.

To illustrate this, recall our discussion of slavery. If one chooses a slave system, that would be a huge gamble. One could win big by being a master or lose badly by being a slave. People looking for the biggest gains will take this risk, but, Rawls says, because this is such an important choice, rational people in the original position will be very conservative. They will not gamble in this way because the costs of losing are too great. To lose and find oneself a slave would be intolerable.

So, the general outcome of the original position deliberations is that people will accept a principle that permits only those inequalities that make the position of the worst off as good as possible. This is precisely what the difference principle does.

A SECOND RAWLSIAN ARGUMENT

Earlier in this chapter, I contrasted the wide-ranging, informal arguments that I have used with the theoretically unified method that Rawls develops through his use of the social contract idea. In addition to his "official" social contract argument for the difference principle, however, Rawls has another informal argument for it. Since this informal argument contains some important ideas, I will briefly describe it here.

When Rawls first introduces the second principle of justice, it does not include the difference principle. It says:

> [S]ocial and economic inequalities are to be arranged so that they are both (a) reasonably expected to be to everyone's advantage, and (b) attached to positions and offices open to all. (60)

The difference principle is introduced later as the proper interpretation of the second principle. Before adopting it, Rawls mentions two other interpretations and explains why he rejects them.

The first interpretation involves what he calls the "system of natural liberty." By this, he means libertarian capitalism, a pure market system. According to this system, any distribution is just as long as (a) it is not the product of force or fraud, and (b) everyone has a right to compete for higher-paying positions. Within this system, having a "right to compete" means that there are no legal prohibitions on eligibility for positions. No one is prohibited by law from competing for positions that carry greater social and economic rewards.

In the system of natural liberty, then, different people compete for positions, and those who win better positions acquire a greater share of resources. No limit is placed on the amount that anyone can acquire. Nor is anyone guaranteed access to any resources.

Rawls rejects this libertarian system because he thinks that the distribution of resources it produces will be too heavily influenced by the

> prior distribution of natural . . . talents and abilities . . . as these have been developed or left unrealized, and their use favored or disfavored . . . by social circumstances[,] . . . accident and good fortune. (72)

Rawls's concern is that if we simply let people compete for resources, then whether people win or lose will be heavily influenced by the natural talents that people have (or lack) plus the beneficial or harmful social circumstances in which people find themselves. Some people are born with traits that will make them good competitors in the market, but others are not. Some are born in social circumstances that are conducive to the development of traits and abilities that will help them succeed, but others are not. Among the fundamental determinants of success and failure, then, will be factors over which people have little or no control, and Rawls thinks this is unjust. As he writes,

> Intuitively, the most obvious injustice of the system of natural liberty is that it permits distributive shares to be improperly influenced by . . . factors [that are] arbitrary from a moral point of view. (72)

Rawls's argument against the system of natural liberty has a good deal of plausibility. Few of us think that the accidents of birth and social circumstance should determine a person's life prospects. That is the way a caste system or hereditary hierarchy works. Yet, the system of natural liberty, Rawls suggests, is morally similar. People do compete and make efforts, but their ability to succeed depends to a great extent on the advantages and disadvantages that they happen to have inherited from nature or acquired from their social circumstances.

FAIR EQUALITY OF OPPORTUNITY

One response to this problem is for society to use its resources to help people prepare to compete in the market. Instead of providing everyone with the merely formal, legal right to compete, proponents of fair equal opportunity acknowledge that everyone should have a fair chance to win. This requires providing all with education, training, and other goods that give them a real chance to succeed in the competition for more favored positions in society.

Rawls does not oppose these steps. He thinks they are necessary, but he does not think they are sufficient to guarantee that the resulting distribution is just. There are two basic reasons for this. First, even if the system succeeds in eliminating the advantages that some get through the social contingencies of being born into a well-off family, "it still permits the distribution of wealth and income to be determined by the natural distribution of abilities and talents" (73–4). Even the most effective program to even out social advantages and disadvantages would leave significant, morally arbitrary factors in place—the advantages and disadvantages that come with genetic makeup. These would still play a very important role in affecting the outcome of economic competition.

The second problem is that the advantages and disadvantages that accompany social contingencies cannot be done away with. This is because the development of natural capacities is so heavily influenced by the family and the social position in which people find themselves. "Even the willingness to make an effort, to try," he says, "is itself dependent upon happy family and social circumstances." (74) As long as we leave the family intact, the advantages and disadvantages of social circumstance cannot be undone. Rawls is emphatic on this point. "It is impossible," he writes, "to secure equal chances of achievement" for all. Rather than denying this fact, he suggests that we "adopt a principle that recognizes this fact and also mitigates the arbitrary effects of the natural lottery itself" (74).[2]

[2] For further discussion of this problem, see James Fishkin, *Justice, Equal Opportunity, and the Family* (New Haven, Conn.: Yale University Press, 1983).

The difference principle succeeds where these fail. It does not make access to resources totally dependent on the contingencies of nature or social circumstance. Taking seriously the moral worth of every member of society, it guarantees a tolerable level of well-being for all. It does this by channeling the distribution of goods through a system that permits inequalities but only insofar as they benefit the worst off. For Rawls, a just society will not simply consign those who cannot compete effectively in the market to an intolerably low status.

IMPLICATIONS FOR THE WELFARE STATE

Rawls's arguments give us another way to understand the moral basis for the welfare state. As we saw earlier, a welfare state is one that provides a legal right to access to at least some resources for all citizens, while at the same time permitting private property, a market system, and some degree of inequality.

Rawls has two main arguments why such a state is required by justice. First, and most important, it is the kind of state that we ourselves would choose if we were in the ideal circumstances of the original position. We would all agree to this kind of society because no matter what position we end up occupying, we will have the same basic liberties as others. In addition, even if we end up in the economically worst off position, the difference principle guarantees that this is the best we could hope for. If inequalities were done away with, our own less good position would be still worse. So, whatever inequalities exist are justified.

Rawls's second, more informal argument gives further support to the claim that a welfare state is superior to a pure market system. A pure market system rewards the winners of economic competition, and we might think that the winners deserve their superior rewards. On reflection, however, it is clear that who wins is heavily influenced by natural and social contingencies, the luck of the draw that determines what our genetically inherited traits are and whether our social situation is conducive to developing the skills and traits necessary for successful competition.

For Rawls, there is nothing unjust about the fact that people acquire different traits or circumstances, but it is unjust if society allows inherited traits and circumstances to determine people's life prospects. As he writes:

> The natural distribution [of inherited traits] is neither just nor unjust; nor is it unjust that men are born into society at some particular position. These are simply natural facts. What is just and unjust is the way that institutions deal with these facts. . . . The social system is not an unchangeable order beyond human control. (102)

It is important, then, that we distinguish the natural order from the social order. While there are some facts of nature that we must simply accept, we do not have to accept social outcomes that are based on natural facts. Instead, we can and should alter social outcomes in accord with the principles of justice. This is what Rawls's theory requires. As he says,

> In justice as fairness men agree to share one another's fate. In designing institutions they undertake to avail themselves of the accidents of nature and social circumstance only when doing so is for the common benefit. The two principles are a fair way of meeting the arbitrariness of fortune. . . . (102)

While Rawls draws on different arguments from the ones I have used, the result of his reflections is extremely friendly to the conclusions I have defended. His criterion of economic justice permits significant economic inequalities, but it permits them only when they are necessary to make the position of the least well off as good as possible. He believes that a just society cannot leave people at the mercy of the marketplace and rejects libertarian capitalism because it permits unjust inequalities. Rawls also gives priority to protecting political and civil liberties. For this reason, he would reject those forms of socialism that have been willing to sacrifice civil and political rights to achieve economic equality. In addition, he rejects socialism because it insists on a stricter form of equality than is actually required by justice. These conclusions are all consistent with my defense of a welfare state, and some form of welfare state seems to be best suited to realizing Rawls's principles.

EVALUATING RAWLSIAN JUSTICE

At the start of this chapter, I suggested that Rawls's theory might help us to do two things: understand more fully the moral basis of the welfare state and begin to determine how much a welfare state should provide for its citizens. Having described the basic components of Rawls's theory, I now want to see how helpful the theory is. My intent is not to provide a complete assessment of Rawls's theory. Instead, I will focus on three questions that are most relevant to my inquiry into the nature of economic justice.

> First, what is the value of Rawls's social contract method?
>
> Second, does the difference principle correctly state the requirements of economic justice?
>
> Third, does Rawls's theory help us to decide what level of resources a just society will provide for its citizens?

THE SOCIAL CONTRACT METHOD

There are two extreme views that might be taken about Rawls's social contract method of argument. According to one view (sometimes suggested by Rawls but never fully embraced), a social contract argument is the only appropriate kind of argument for defending principles of justice. The opposite extreme view is that social contract arguments are artificial, irrelevant, and unhelpful.[3]

[3] For criticism of the social contract method, see Ronald Dworkin, "The Original Position," in Norman Daniels, ed., *Reading Rawls* (New York: Basic Books, 1975). For brief, helpful remarks on methods of argument, see Will Kymlicka, *Contemporary Political Philosophy* (Oxford: Oxford University Press, 1990), ch. 1.

My own view is that the social contract argument is one form of argument we can draw on and that we should use it along with others. While it is not absolutely necessary to inquiries about justice, neither is it pointless or irrelevant.

Why is the social contract method not necessary? Because there are many kinds of arguments that people give to defend views about justice, and any argument that can be seen to have a point merits consideration. Arguments need not take any specific form. They may appeal to general principles, or they may appeal to examples of just or unjust practices. They may invoke historical experience, economic theories, or theories of human nature. Indeed, they may emerge from novels, stories, plays, and even from jokes and songs. Anything that seems relevant should be examined, whether it is cast in the form of a social contract argument or not.

To say this, however, is not to denigrate the contract method. Rawls's theory is, I think, very helpful in thinking about problems of economic justice. It is helpful in part because it changes our perspective in useful ways. All of us are used to a certain repertoire of slogans and arguments about wealth and poverty, justice and injustice. Often, when we engage in political and moral debate, we quickly settle into familiar ruts and simply reproduce the slogans and arguments we have heard before. We need ways to free ourselves from rigid, ritualized forms of thought, and Rawls's social contract method can help us do that.

In addition, since all of us have vested interests either in change or in the preservation of the current order, our reasoning may be influenced by concerns about our own personal well-being. While we know that the fact that an arrangement benefits ourselves is not strictly relevant to deciding whether it is just or unjust, we may nonetheless be influenced in our judgments by concerns about our own well-being.

Rawls's contract method is helpful in two ways. First, by requiring a different kind of thought exercise, it helps us get out of the ruts of conventional thinking and thus makes possible a fresh view. Second, by imposing the veil of ignorance, it prevents us from giving too much weight to the advantages or disadvantages that we personally derive from our current institutions. It forces us to argue in ways that give equal weight to everyone's well-being.

That our thinking about justice can be contaminated by concern for our own interests is powerfully brought out by the nineteenth century economist, Jean-Baptiste Say. He writes:

> Persons, who under a vicious order of things have obtained a competent share of social enjoyments, are never in want of arguments to justify . . . such a state of society. . . . If the same individuals were tomorrow required to cast anew the lots assigning them a place in society, they would find many things to object to.[4]

Say brings out the relation between our degree of personal contentment with a social system and our belief about whether the system is just. We feel

[4] Quoted in G.A. Cohen, "Robert Nozick and Wilt Chamberlain: How Patterns Preserve Liberty," in J. Arthur and W. Shaw, eds. *Justice and Economic Distribution*, 2nd ed. (Englewood Cliffs, N.J." Prentice Hall, 1991), 212.

that a social order is justifiable because it is fine for us. Say makes this vivid by imagining a lottery to assign new places. As he correctly notes, people's attitudes toward a system might well change if they could not count on retaining an advantageous position within it.[5]

The same kind of unsettling effect is produced by Rawls's thought experiment and by the prospect of renegotiating the social contract from a position of ignorance about our own situation. Whatever its faults, the method has inspired a great deal of new thinking. One can praise it for its fruitfulness without thinking it is the only legitimate form of social thought.

THE DIFFERENCE PRINCIPLE AND ECONOMIC JUSTICE

The difference principle is at the heart of Rawls's answer to the question of what constitutes a just economic order. It tells us that economic inequalities are acceptable only if they maximize the life prospects of the worst-off group (e.g., unskilled workers). From one perspective, this can be seen as a permissive view, since it allows some people to possess more than others. Nonetheless, it is restrictive because it makes disparities in possessions depend on their being advantageous to the least well-off people. Disparities that do not improve the lot of the least well off are unjust.

Given this mix of features, Rawls may have hoped that the difference principle would be accepted both by egalitarians and anti-egalitiarians. Egalitarians should see that the difference principle actually makes people better off than they would be with a purely equal distribution, while anti-egalitarians should be pleased that Rawls defends inequalities that provide incentives for greater productivity. In fact, however, the difference principle has been attacked by both sides.

To see why egalitarians would reject the difference principle, consider the following choice:

	Situation E	**Situation F**
Group A	250	275
Group B	250	2750

In considering this case, I want to assume three things. First, the initial situation E is rather bad; people with 250 units of resources live a difficult and unpleasant life. Second, moving up to 275 units of resources in situation F still leaves people rather badly off. Third, I assume that the move from E to F satisfies the difference principle, that permitting less than 2750 for members of group B would leave members of group A with less than 275.

Why would egalitarians reject the move from E to F? After all, it does make the least well-off people better off.

[5] For a similar point about the influence of uncertainty on judgment, see Robert Goodin, *Motivating Political Morality* (Cambridge, Mass.: Blackwell, 1992), chap. 3.

In spite of the improvement of group A's standard of living, their lives in situation F have features that are undesirable. Given the large-scale differences in resources between members of A and B, people in group B may now have sources of power that were previously unavailable to them. They may acquire, for example, the ability to hire and fire people, thus giving them economic power over others and a potential for domination they previously lacked. In addition, by controlling more resources, they have greater power to determine how resources are invested and hence in what direction the society will move. Finally, they may possess greater political influence than they had before, thus opening the way for other forms of domination that did not exist before. So, even though the move from E to F improves the economic situation of less well-off people, it creates inequalities of power that will be troubling to egalitarians.

This egalitarian criticism is important and should carry weight even for those of us who are not strict egalitarians. We should see that an economically better off society might have power relations that make it less just overall than a poorer, but more equal society.

Readers familiar with Rawls's theory may think that his first principle of justice, the equal liberty principle, would rule out the move from E to F. If this is so, then a combination of the first and second principles would be sufficient for dealing with the egalitarian's objection. I believe, however, that the first principle, as Rawls himself understands it, permits inequalities of actual political power so long as people have formal or legal equality in the political realm. For example, the first principle seems to permit a situation in which everyone has a right to vote and run for office, even though wealthy people can use their money to acquire more political influence than poorer people.[6]

Whether or not Rawls himself would accept the egalitarian argument against moving from E to F, one point is clear. In determining whether an economic arrangement is just, we need to look beyond the distribution of money and other economic resources. We need to look as well at how power and influence are distributed in a society. An arrangement can be unjust if it gives some people inordinate control over the lives of others.[7] What this objection shows is that a distribution can have this defect, even if it satisfies the difference principle.

Now consider an objection that anti-egalitarians would raise against the difference principle. This objection begins by considering the following situations:

	Situation G	**Situation H**
Group A	2250	2250
Group B	2250	22,500

[6] On this point, see Rawls, *A Theory of Justice,* 204. For a valuable critical discussion of this issue, see Norman Daniels, "Equal Liberty and Unequal Worth of Liberty," in Norman Daniels, ed. *Reading Rawls* (New York: Basic Books, 1975).

[7] This point is stressed by Michael Walzer in *Spheres of Justice* (New York: Basic Books, 1983).

In considering the justice of these distributions, I will make three assumptions. First, I assume that the situation of groups A and B in situation G is quite good. The 2250 units of resources that all possess is sufficient for a decent life. Second, I assume that the political system in situation H is designed so that money cannot be used to acquire political influence. Thus, the fact that members of group B have more resources does not mean that they have a greater say in social decisions than members of group A. Third, the major benefit to group B in situation H is that they are able to purchase various luxury items; they do not, however, have either political or social power over others.

Given these (perhaps unrealistic) assumptions, what shall we say about the move from G to H? First, it is clear that this move would not satisfy the difference principle. According to the difference principle, H is unjust because it permits inequalities that fail to improve the situation of the less well-off people.

Nonetheless, it is not evident that situation H is unjust. Nor is it clear that people in the original position should reject it. Why is this?

First, even though the move from G to H creates a large economic inequality and even though it does nothing to improve the lot of group A, their economic situation is rather good in both situations. They are not in dire need, and the improvement for group B does not worsen conditions for members of group A.

Second, I have assumed that increased wealth does not buy increased power for group B. Because the political system is designed to prevent the influence of money on elections and policy choices, the economic inequality does not produce political inequality. In addition, since members of group A have a decent standard of living, they need not accept jobs on bad terms and thus cannot be exploited by members of group B.

For these reasons, I believe that the move from G to H can be just, and I conclude that a distribution can be just, even if it violates the difference principle.

SOME MORALS OF THE STORY

If we put together these objections, two important points emerge. First, whether an inequality is just or unjust depends in part on whether the situation of the worst off is good or bad. If it is bad, then inequalities may be suspect. If it is good, then the fact that other people have more may not be a problem.

At the start of this book, I claimed that problems of economic justice arose in part because of huge disparities in resources. What we can now see is that it is not the disparities themselves that are unjust. What is unjust is the existence of these disparities in situations in which those with less are very badly off, while those with more enjoy access to luxuries. If all are decently off, then economic inequalities may not be unjust. That some people enjoy luxuries is only unjust if others (through no fault of their own) lack access to necessities.

In saying this, I do not mean to exclude the possibility that great wealth and large economic disparities might be morally criticizable on grounds other than justice. One might think that it is simply morally offensive that some people should live at such levels of opulence. Or one might think that great wealth must corrupt people's character, that good character is incompatible with the ability to satisfy so many of one's desires. It is not uncommon to hear of wealthy people who have earned their riches and who then worry that their children will be worthless people who simply take wealth for granted. So, I do not mean to settle the question whether great wealth is morally bad or wrong. I do want to say, however, that under certain conditions, it need not constitute an injustice. For this reason, a society need not prohibit great wealth and economic disparities in order to be a just society.

The second key point is that whether an economic inequality is just or unjust depends on the further effects of economic inequality. Typically, greater economic resources bring with them greater political and economic power. If the political system could be shielded from economic influence, however, that would remove one of the reasons for thinking that economic inequalities are unjust. Likewise, if the situation of all is relatively good, then the least well-off people will not be vulnerable to economic exploitation. People only take badly paying, unpleasant, unsafe jobs if they are desperate. If no one were desperate, no one would be forced to take such jobs.

How do these conclusions compare with Rawls's principles?

First, from a strictly economic perspective, the view I have stated is less egalitarian than Rawls's. It permits economic inequalities that do not benefit the least well off. It only does this, however, when (a) the situation of the worst off is good, and (b) greater economic resources cannot be used to create inequalities of political and economic power.

Second, the points I have made about economic and political power are not stressed by Rawls in connection with the difference principle. He does not stress the importance of the forms of power that resources can buy. Nonetheless, what I have said could be understood as a development of Rawls's first principle of justice, the equal liberty principle. As many have argued, extreme inequalities of wealth can lead to diminished liberty for those who have less. Thus a robust interpretation of the first principle could be used to defend economic equality as a requirement for achieving political equality.

This leads to two conclusions about the justice of economic inequalities.

1. Economic inequalities can be just (even if they do not satisfy the difference principle) if (a) all are at a decent level of well-being, and (b) steps can be taken to prevent people from using more wealth to generate increased political and economic power.

2. If increased wealth cannot be prevented from bringing with it increased political and economic power, then economic inequalities will be unjust, even if they satisfy the difference principle.

SUMMING UP

Looking back over this chapter, what can we say about the helpfulness of Rawls's theory?

First, while Rawls's social contract method is not a necessary form for arguments about justice to take, it is a useful kind of argument. All too often, we argue in ruts and are too influenced by our own position in society. It is worth asking whether we would be as content with our institutions if we were to occupy the position of the least well-off people in our society.

Second, Rawls draws our attention to the connections between political and economic justice. We cannot say whether a society is just if we confine our attention simply to the formal political rights of people or to the distribution of economic goods. We need to examine both aspects of a society. This is a point that both libertarian capitalists and state socialists have often failed to address.

Third, Rawls is correct to emphasize the importance of people being provided with education and other goods that enable them to compete for positions within society. Equal opportunity cannot be limited to the legal right to compete for positions. People must have access to some level of resources if they are to have a genuine opportunity to compete for social and economic rewards. Providing people with this level of opportunity is an important function of a welfare state.

Fourth, the difference principle rightly draws our attention to the well-being of the least well off as a test for the justice of a distribution. Unfortunately, it oversimplifies things. By focusing only on the inequality between the well off and the least advantaged, Rawls overlooks the fact that inequalities matter more in some situations than in others. If the least well off are at a good level and if additional resources for the well off do not allow them to dominate others, either politically or economically, then economic disparities are harmless and not unjust. As a result, a society can fail to satisfy the difference principle and yet be just. Likewise, a society can meet the requirements of the difference principle and yet be unjust because it permits political domination or economic exploitation.

Overall, then, while Rawls's theory contains many points of great value, the difference principle is not an adequate criterion for determining whether a distribution of social and economic goods is just.

CHAPTER NINE

What Should Welfare States Provide?

In the United States, the welfare state has been subject to severe attack. Yet, on reflection, it seems clear that some form of welfare state is superior either to pure market capitalism or to state socialism.

I base this conclusion on the fact that when we compare these systems from the perspective of three central values, the welfare state emerges as the clear winner. It does a better job of promoting human well-being than its competitors, a better job of giving people what they deserve (both in terms of personal desert and human desert), and a better job of promoting both positive and negative liberty, assuring people both freedom from interference and the ability to promote their own well-being.

In addition, Rawls's social contract theory provides further support for the welfare state. It suggests that a welfare state would be agreed to by persons in an ideal choosing situation.[1] People in Rawls's "original position" would not choose either libertarian capitalism or the strict economic equality that socialists aim for. They would not choose a society that would leave them entirely at the mercy of the state or the market.

HOW MUCH "WELFARE"?

While the case for some form of welfare state is very strong, we still need to decide what resources such a state ought to distribute to citizens and under what circumstances it should assume this role. How we answer these questions

[1] For an interesting discussion that interprets Rawls somewhat differently, see R. Krouse and M. McPherson, "Capitalism, 'Property-Owning Democracy,' and the Welfare State," in A. Gutman ed., *Democracy and the Welfare State* (Princeton, N.J.: Princeton University Press, 1988), 79–105.

will determine the type of welfare state we favor. Should government play a minimal role in distributing goods? Or should it play an extensive role? Should state distribution of resources be a last resort, a backup that is used only in emergency situations? Or should it be a regular feature of normal life?

These questions about the extent of the welfare state underlie many current political controversies. Three basic issues are involved in these debates:

1. What goods should the state distribute?
2. How much of these goods should it distribute?
3. Who should receive these goods?

I want to work toward an answer to these questions by describing two very different kinds of welfare states and seeing what can be said for and against them. As before, the states I describe are "ideal types" rather than actual existing institutions. The virtue of these idealizations is that their logic is clearer than real institutions, and this makes it easier to think about them. Once we have assessed these simpler models, we can apply our results to the actual institutions and practices that we find in the world.

THE EMERGENCY RELIEF STATE

The first kind of welfare state I want to consider is a very minimal form of welfare state. It is based on the idea that the state should limit its role to providing emergency relief to people in conditions of extreme distress. In this kind of state, almost all goods would be distributed through the market and private gift giving, but in extreme situations, these would be supplemented by government distribution.

The emergency relief state (as I am conceiving it) would provide goods to citizens only when their lack of resources threatens them either with loss of life or severe injury. So, for example, a person on the verge of death by starvation would be provided with food. A person threatened with death or severe injury from the cold would be provided with temporary shelter. In this model, welfare state activities would be a form of individualized, emergency disaster relief. They would be temporary, unusual, and restricted to people in the direst of situations.

The emergency relief form of welfare state incorporates the following answers to our three questions.

1. What resources should the state distribute? Just those goods needed to prevent death or severe injury.
2. How much of these goods should it distribute? Just the amount of those goods needed to prevent death or serious injury.
3. Who should receive these goods? Just those people who are in dire need of them and who cannot purchase them or acquire them as gifts.

The emergency relief state may strike some people as too meager to be called a genuine welfare state. Nonetheless, it is a genuine welfare state because it rejects the principle that all goods should be distributed according to market value and gifts. In this form of state, citizens have a legal right to emergency relief, something they would not have in a pure libertarian capitalist order. In addition, the emergency relief state has just those features that libertarians object to: It goes beyond providing citizens with police protection and uses taxes to pay for the emergency resources it provides.

How should we evaluate this form of welfare state? We can do this by comparing it with a pure system of market capitalism, using the main criteria I have appealed to before: well-being, desert, and liberty. Drawing on my previous arguments, I will sketch an answer that I think is plausible.

Well-being. The emergency relief state is likely to do better in promoting well-being than a pure market system because it will prevent substantial forms of harm and suffering. The resources used to do this will be taken in taxes, but they will do so much good for the recipients (preventing death and extreme injury) that it is very unlikely that more good could be done with the same money by those whose taxes support this activity. In addition, the costs of emergency relief can be spread among many people, thus minimizing the sacrifice required to provide substantial gains for those in need.

Finally, because the emergency relief state responds only to dire suffering, it will not undermine anyone's incentive to work productively. People who receive this aid must still meet virtually all of their needs by themselves. Even after receiving this aid, they will not be well off and will still have a strong incentive to work in order to improve their situation.

Desert. If we believe that people deserve some kind of decent treatment simply as human beings, then the emergency relief state does a better job of giving people what they deserve than does a pure market system. A pure market system has no room for "human" desert as the basis for a claim to any social resources. While libertarians do not seek to deprive people of goods, neither do they believe that anyone deserves to have any of their needs met by others. If we believe that this form of human desert exists (and that it underlies the right not to be killed or tortured, for example), then we are likely to think that people in dire need deserve a humane response from people who are well off. In addition, as citizens, such people deserve some level of concern from their own government, which is supposed to represent them and defend their interests. Because total indifference to people in dire need does not show the kind of consideration they deserve, the emergency relief state is superior to a pure market system.

While this state does require taxes from people, we have seen that a market system does not distribute goods according to desert. Therefore, in taking some resources from people, we are not depriving them of things they personally deserve by virtue of effort and contribution. Much of what people acquire in a market system is not personally deserved. It is a function of luck, return on investments, inheritance, and other factors not connected to their own efforts and contributions. In addition, even when people do work hard at worthwhile tasks, it is often impossible to determine just how much credit is theirs (as opposed to others involved in the same tasks). There is no way to say precisely how much of a reward they deserve for their personal efforts.

Liberty. While a libertarian capitalist system honors people's negative liberty by not inflicting evils upon them, it ignores the claims of positive liberty. It takes no interest in enhancing people's ability to satisfy their needs and desires or carry out their plans. By intervening to prevent death and injury, the emergency relief state increases positive liberty. It provides people with the resources needed to live and sustain their physical and mental capacities. It tides people over until they can try to achieve their goals on their own. Hence, the emergency relief state promotes liberty better than a pure market society.

Granted, it does curtail the liberty of the well off by taxing them, thereby depriving them of the ability to do some things that they might want to do. Nonetheless, because the well off already have a great deal of positive liberty (having resources that enable them to act on many desires and intentions), greater overall liberty is promoted by funneling some resources in the direction of people in dire straits. As with the argument about well-being, a greater value (more liberty) is achieved by directing resources from the well off to those in dire need.

Finally, if we supplement these three values by appealing to Rawls's social contract method of reasoning, it is plausible to conclude that people who did not know their own position in society would choose a system that provides emergency relief over one that does not guarantee access to any resources. If people were faced with the choice of having a relief system in place or relying on the contingencies of charity and if they did not know whether they would be needy or well off, it would be rational for them to choose a society that provides emergency relief to all who need it. People who reject the emergency relief state may be influenced by their own confidence that they will not need its assistance. If they were behind the "veil of ignorance" and did not know this, their view would probably be different.

For all these reasons, then, the emergency relief type of welfare state appears to be superior to a pure market system.

LIMITATIONS OF THE EMERGENCY RELIEF STATE

While the emergency relief state is better than no welfare state at all, it has severe limitations, and if we accept the goals of promoting well-being, rewarding desert, and promoting liberty, it is difficult to see how we could be content with the limited goals of the emergency relief state. There are several reasons for this.

First, if we are genuinely concerned with promoting people's well-being, it does not make sense to limit the state to emergency relief. Since emergency situations often arise out of chronic problems, we can often provide more effective assistance by taking preventative measures rather than waiting until people are on the verge of death or severe injury. It makes sense, for example, to provide people an adequate supply of food rather than to wait for them to be dying of starvation. It makes sense to help people find shelter rather than to wait for them to be dying from exposure. It makes sense to immunize people against disease rather than to wait for them to fall ill.

Indeed, if we only intervene in emergencies, it is hard to see how people in need will get themselves to a position of genuine well-being. If we provide only emergency relief, people are likely to be in need of emergency relief over and over again, while if we are more generous in what we provide, we may lift them to a level where they are less likely to be vulnerable again.

There is, then, a kind of inefficiency in the emergency relief strategy. By limiting the resources it provides so severely, it fails to attack problems of suffering and deprivation in an effective way.

Second, if we want to maximize well-being, it is doubtful that we do so by limiting state-provided resources so severely. People who are successfully protected from death and injury may still be badly off, while well-off people may still have vast resources that go well beyond providing what they want or need. So, there is no reason to believe that we make the best use of resources by limiting what the state provides to emergency relief.

Even if we are concerned about leaving intact both the positive and the negative incentives to work and even if we subtract the losses in well-being that occur because of taxation, channeling a greater amount of resources to less well-off people than the emergency relief state provides seems likely to produce greater benefits.

As a result, even though the emergency relief state promotes well-being more effectively than a pure market economy, it is unlikely that it promotes well-being as effectively as possible. A more extensive provision of resources to less well-off people would do more good, since emergency relief alone will leave people severely deprived even after receiving it. As a result, anyone concerned about promoting well-being is unlikely to be happy with this minimalist version of the welfare state.

The same result follows if we are concerned about treating people as they humanly deserve. If we take seriously the idea that every person has an inherent moral value and, therefore, deserves to be treated decently and humanely, then we will not think that the emergency relief state succeeds in giving people the consideration they deserve. While it does act to spare them from death and severe injury, it stands by while they suffer deprivations that are less than life threatening and less than severely injurious. If we think that people deserve decent treatment, we will not be content with a system that waits for them to be in the direst of situations before intervening on their behalf. Instead, we will favor earlier intervention to prevent them from being in such terrible situations.

To see why this is plausible, consider these remarks by Amartya Sen about the availability of food in India. He writes:

> There has been no famine in post-independence India, but perhaps a third of India's rural population is perennially undernourished. . . . The elimination of famines coexists with the survival of widespread "regular hunger." The right to

"adequate means" of *nourishment* does not at all seem to arouse political concern in a way that the right to "adequate means" to *avoid starvation* does."[2]

If we think that all people deserve humane treatment, it is hard to see how to justify a policy that helps them avoid starvation but leaves them chronically malnourished. Of course, preventing starvation is better than nothing, and if resource limitations prevent greater assistance, this policy would be legitimate. However, if more assistance is possible and if our aim is to treat people as they humanly deserve, it makes no sense to rest content with a system that prevents starvation but permits malnutrition. To be indifferent to chronic malnutrition shows no less disrespect for people than to be indifferent to starvation.

A concern to treat all people as they humanly deserve, then, will lead to dissatisfaction with the limited provisions of the emergency relief state. If we are genuinely concerned about treating people decently and humanely, we will favor doing more.

Finally, the same point applies to the promotion of liberty. While saving people from death and injury does contribute to their capacities to live and act, providing them with a more constant source of resources would increase their capacities even more. So, if we accept the argument from positive liberty to justify emergency relief, the logic of that argument will lead us beyond the emergency relief state to a more extensive welfare state, one that provides people with sufficient resources to prevent their being in dire straits to begin with. To return to Sen's example, while we increase positive liberty by preventing people from starving, we can increase it even more by providing them with enough food to overcome chronic malnutrition, since this condition severely diminishes their capacity in many ways.

The arguments for the emergency relief state, then, are unstable. They show its superiority to a pure market system, but they strongly suggest that a more ambitious form of welfare state would be better. But how ambitious should such a state be? How much more than emergency relief should a welfare state provide?

THE COMPREHENSIVE WELFARE STATE

A second answer to these questions is provided by what I will call the "comprehensive" welfare state. Such a state is dedicated to the goal of ensuring that every citizen has the resources needed to live a decent life.

The comprehensive form of the welfare state embodies the following answers to our three questions.

1. What resources should the state distribute? Those goods that are needed to live a decent life.

[2] "Property and Hunger," in J. Arthur and W. Shaw, eds., *Social and Political Philosophy* (Englewood Cliffs, N.J.: Prentice Hall, 1992), 229. Originally published in *Economics and Philosophy* 4 (1988).

2. How much of these goods should it distribute? The amount of those goods that is required for living a decent life.
3. Who should receive these goods? Everyone.

The basic idea underlying this conception of the welfare state is that a society cannot be just so long as (a) some people lack the resources required for a decent life and (b) the society is sufficiently affluent to provide these resources.

A comprehensive welfare state could operate in different ways. It could provide specific resources such as food, housing, health care, and education to people. Or it could provide enough money to purchase the amount of goods needed for a decent life. Or it could combine these in diverse ways. If income is distributed, it might be supplemented by publicly funded insurance coverage to pay for medical care and other special needs. All citizens would be entitled to this level of income or to the guaranteed allotment. Whatever strategy is adopted, these practices would be a very extensive form of welfare state. I call it a "comprehensive" state because it provides access to a wide range of goods in a regular way to all citizens.[3]

In my discussion of this model, I will not distinguish between states that provide citizens with an income that is sufficient for a decent level of well-being and states that provide citizens with a package of specific goods (food, shelter, education, health care, etc.). What these forms of welfare state have in common is more important than what separates them. They share a commitment to provide citizens with the resources that are required to have a decent life. If this form of state is morally justified, the specific means for achieving its goals can be worked out.

ISN'T THIS SOCIALISM?

Just as the first reaction to the emergency relief model might be that it is too meager to qualify as a welfare state, so the first reaction to the comprehensive model may be that it is simply a form of state socialism and not a welfare state at all. It is important to see why this reaction is mistaken. The comprehensive welfare state may look like socialism, but it is not.

In the comprehensive welfare state, every citizen has a right to a relatively generous minimum share of resources. Nonetheless, there could still be inequalities because other citizens may possess considerably more resources than the basic minimum. In addition, there could still be private ownership of the "means of production" and a market system of production and distribution of most goods. The comprehensive welfare state is a market system with a guaranteed "floor" of income or goods, a level below which no one would fall. Unlike an egalitarian socialist state, however, there would be no "ceiling," no upper limit on how much people may possess.

[3] For a discussion of such a proposal, see R. Theobald, ed., *The Guaranteed Income* (Garden City, N.Y.: Anchor Doubleday, 1967). For a more recent defense of a guaranteed income, see Michael Kinsley, "The Ultimate Block Grant," *The New Yorker,* May 29, 1995, 36–40.

To see that access to a relatively generous allotment of a resource need not entail socialism, consider the case of education in the United States. Education is a welfare good, a resource that is available to all citizens as a matter of legal right and that is distributed by the state. People have a legal right to an education (at least to a certain level), even if they cannot pay for it and even if no one would give it to them as a gift. The cost of education is paid for by taxation.

In the United States, the system of public education coexists with a system of private education. Citizens have a right to attend publicly funded schools, but they are not required to do so. If they wish, they may purchase education privately from nongovernmental schools. In addition, the system permits inequalities in education. If people can purchase either more education or a better education than is provided by public schools, they may do so. So public education enforces a "floor" (a minimum level) for all, but does not enforce a "ceiling" (an upper limit on the amount or quality of education).

The example of education shows that one can have an extensive welfare state without having socialism. Just as public education coexists with privately purchased education and with education of varying degrees of quality, so too a comprehensive welfare state could coexist with an extensive market economy, private ownership of most businesses and industries, and substantial inequalities in the distribution of wealth. Indeed, even if all education were distributed equally by the government (by forbidding both private schools and inequalities in the amount and quality of educational resources), the production and distribution of many other goods could still be carried out through private, market institutions.

People who think that the comprehensive welfare state is a form of socialism mistakenly think that we face an either/or choice between capitalist market institutions and state socialist planning as the sole means of production and distribution in a society. In fact, societies can be (and indeed all are) medleys of diverse means for producing and distributing different goods and services. The virtues of capitalist markets can be retained for many goods, even if the state plays an active role in distributing others. Some goods may be guaranteed to citizens, while others are distributed in accord with ability to pay.

IN DEFENSE OF THE COMPREHENSIVE WELFARE STATE

Many people who believe that the state should provide goods to people as a last resort nonetheless oppose the idea that the state should provide such goods, especially in generous amounts, in a routine fashion. As I have already suggested, however, the very same reasons that support the welfare state (rather than a pure market system) show that a comprehensive welfare state is superior to a minimalist emergency relief state or to any state that provides less than what is needed for a decent level of well-being.

Promoting well-being. In order to promote well-being most effectively, we need to estimate how much good is produced for those who receive resources and how much the well-being of those who pay taxes is diminished. The level of resources we choose will be the one that provides the greatest balance of benefits over losses. In making these calculations, we need to keep in mind that tax payers and recipients are not two separate classes of people. A tax payer may benefit from public education, safe roads, or health insurance, for example. While there will be some people who will simply be recipients and not contributors, virtually all contributors will also benefit in various ways.

There is, of course, no way to determine in the abstract the exact levels of benefits and taxes that will maximize well-being. Nonetheless, we can make plausible judgments about the level of goods that a comprehensive welfare state ought to provide.

My view is that a state that is concerned with promoting well-being will guarantee a decent level to all. Why is this? Because however we specify what a decent level is, anything less will involve some form of serious deprivation. Hence it will tend to diminish the overall level of well-being of individuals and of society generally. If this deprivation coexists with the possession of a substantial surplus for some people, enabling them to live well above a decent level of well-being, then it is likely that taxation of the very well off, while it will diminish their ability to purchase luxuries, will not seriously diminish their level of well-being.

This argument for a comprehensive welfare state depends on the concept of marginal utility discussed in chapter 4. Resources do the most good when they prevent people from being seriously deprived. Hence, it will almost always do more good to transfer resources from those well above a decent level to those below it. As long as people lack the means for a decent level of well-being, it is unlikely that resources are being used to produce the most well-being possible.

This claim is supported by facts about the distribution of wealth and income in the United States. As things stand, a small part of the population has a disproportionate share of income and wealth. ("Income" means the amount earned in a year, while "wealth" means the total assets owned by someone.) In 1989, the top 20 percent of households had about 55 percent of the total income earned in the United States, while the bottom 80 percent took in about 45 percent of total income. One-fifth of families had well over half the total income. If we look at wealth, the inequalities are even larger. In 1989, the top 20 percent held about 94 percent of the total wealth, while the bottom 80 percent possessed only 6 percent. The top 1 percent of families owned 48 percent of the total wealth.[4]

	% of Income	**% of Wealth**
Top 1%	16.47	48.17
Next 19%	39.02	45.76
Bottom 80%	44.52	6.07

[4] These figures from the *Survey of Consumer Finances* appear in Edward N. Wolff, *Top Heavy: A Study of the Increasing Inequality of Wealth in America* (New York: Twentieth Century Fund Press, 1995), 11.

Given these vast disparities and the concentrations of wealth in a small part of the population, the claim that more good could be done with this wealth through transfers to others would appear difficult to dispute.

This is not to say that all inequalities in income or wealth are inherently wrong. Once everyone is guaranteed a decent level of well-being, there is nothing unjust about some people having more money to increase their personal well-being. The effective promotion of well-being does not require either perfect equality or special efforts aimed at diminishing disparities between people. If the extra resources of the wealthy benefit them but do not worsen the situation of others to the point of serious deprivation, there should be no objection to the fact that the wealthy possess luxuries.

The possession of luxuries is morally objectionable only if others are not at a decent level. By providing a decent level to all, the comprehensive welfare state makes luxuries and inequalities morally permissible. Conversely, as long as some are below the level of a decent life, the possession of large surpluses by others is not justifiable.

Some one might object at this point that the idea of a comprehensive welfare state is flawed because the notion of a "decent level" of well-being is hopelessly vague. It does not tell us what level of well-being should be provided to people by the state.

I agree that this is a vague notion, but I do not think that it can or should be made more specific at this point in the discussion. What counts as a decent level of well-being varies in different times and places. It is not fixed once and for all time, even though some necessities like food will remain constant as part of different conceptions of decency. The theory of economic justice tells us that people should have access to the resources required for a decent level of well-being, but the theory itself cannot tell us what those specific resources are.

When we move from the level of theory to questions about what resources to distribute in a particular society, then we both can and must give more specific content to the idea of a "decent" level of well-being for that particular society. We can do this by considering the resources that are available to the society as a whole, the kind of life led by people in that society, and the beliefs of people in the society about what constitutes a decent life.

The list of resources needed for a "decent" level of well-being both varies among societies and depends in part on people's beliefs and values. The specific criteria for a decent life are rooted in what Michael Walzer has called the "shared understandings" of a society.[5] For this reason, the idea of "decency" is partly subjective, since it varies with people's beliefs. Nonetheless, because the idea of a decent life is a social concept, we can construct a relatively objective test of decency. We can define a decent level of well-being in a particular society as the level of well-being that most people in that society regard as decent. As standards change, so will people's sense of what is necessary to live a decent

[5] For this view about the nature of goods, see Michael Walzer, *Spheres of Justice* (New York: Basic Books, 1983), 6–10.

life. What the level is can be determined by studying people's attitudes and by seeing the role that different resources play in people's lives.

We might ask, for example, whether owning a telephone is required for a decent life in our society. Most of the people who have had decent lives throughout history have lacked telephones. Being deprived of a telephone in our society, however, has a very different impact on life than being deprived of a telephone a century ago. For this reason, it is possible that people in our society would see a telephone as an essential part of a decent life, since it is required for communicating with people in ways that members of our society take for granted. If people do see a telephone as necessary for a decent life in our society, then a comprehensive welfare state would provide people with adequate resources for having telephone service. If it is not seen as necessary, it need not be provided.

To take a more pressing example, if we determine that adequate medical care is part of a decent level of well-being, we will have to determine just what level of care is required. This will depend, in part, on what resources a society possesses and how much of its total resources it wants to devote to medical care as opposed to other needs, like education, transportation, defense, or the arts. In addition, however, it will be determined by what sorts of treatments are thought to be required for a decent life and what sorts are seen as luxuries to which people are not automatically entitled.

The key point is that a society that is concerned about promoting social well-being will aim to provide all citizens with whatever goods they need to live a decent life. What those goods are, however, cannot be specified apart from a knowledge of the conditions in that society and people's beliefs about what constitutes a decent life.

Desert. I argued earlier that a concern to treat people as they humanly deserve would favor an emergency relief state rather than a pure market economy. Then, I claimed that if we are moved by this argument, its logic will impel us toward a more extensive form of welfare state. Indeed, if we regard all people as deserving of decent and humane treatment, we will conclude that the society to which they belong ought to take a serious interest in their well-being. My claim here is that if a society is able to provide a decent level of well-being for all its citizens and chooses not to do so, then it is failing to treat them in a fully humane way. A commitment to treating all as they deserve will lead to a decision to provide them with the resources necessary for a decent well-being if this is possible.

Suppose, however, that a person squanders the resources provided by the state and as a result can no longer sustain a decent level of well-being. Doesn't that show, one might ask, that the task of providing someone with a decent level of well-being is impossible? Aren't people responsible for their own well-being?

This objection rests on a misunderstanding. In treating people as they deserve, we need not and cannot make them well off or happy. If they misuse resources, harm themselves, or are simply unlucky in areas of their life, that does not show that they have been treated poorly by society. What the comprehensive welfare state provides are the *resources* necessary for a decent life. It cannot guarantee, however, that any individual will be happy or that everyone will use these resources effectively. What it will ensure, however, is that the setbacks a person suffers will not be caused by a lack of access to basic resources. Once that level is guaranteed, it becomes true that people are responsible for their own fates. Without access to these resources, however, this cannot be said of them.

A second objection suggests that people do in fact deserve their individual fates and that those who lack resources have simply failed to do what is necessary to raise themselves to a decent level.

This objection may apply to some people, but it is important to see how many people it does not apply to. It does not apply to children, whose powers have not developed and who cannot be expected to maintain themselves or faulted for having less than adequate resources. It does not apply to older people whose capacities for supporting themselves may have diminished over time. Finally, it does not apply to people who are set back by illness, disabilities, and natural disasters. None of these people can be said to deserve a lower status in the economic order.

To return to the statistics on wealth distribution given above, it is implausible in the extreme to think that the 80 percent of families who possess only 6 percent of total wealth deserve such a small share of the resources of society. Nor is it plausible to believe that the top 1 percent fully deserve the 48 percent of total wealth that they possess.

Undeserved wealth need not be unjust and may be permitted by a comprehensive welfare state. Undeserved poverty, however, is an injustice, and preventing it is a central goal of a comprehensive welfare state.

Liberty. The comprehensive welfare state promotes liberty in three different ways. First, by providing each person with the resources necessary for a decent level of well-being, it protects people from the incapacities that result from a lack of resources. People without food, shelter, medical care, and education (to name some basic goods) are incapacitated by these lacks. They are unable to take the steps necessary to achieve their goals. They lack the positive liberties possessed by people who have these resources. Hence, providing access to these resources directly promotes their liberty.

Second, access to these resources enhances liberty by making people invulnerable to exploitation. People who lack the resources for a decent life may be forced to accept jobs that are unduly burdensome and unhealthy or that pay so poorly that they do not enable people to lead a decent life. Because such people are in a weak position to bargain for better pay and better working conditions, they are highly vulnerable to exploitation. Like the person confronted with the thief's "your money or your life," the person without resources may be forced to accept options that no one would ever voluntarily choose. The comprehensive welfare state protects people by enabling them to reject unacceptable work situations.

As things stand, many people do not have the liberty to say no, and their lack of liberty is exploited to produce benefits for others. As John Kenneth Galbraith points out,

> [T]he poor in our economy . . . do the work that the more fortunate do not do and would find manifestly distasteful, even distressing.[6]

The distasteful work done by the poor is not incidental to the well-being of better-off people. Galbraith emphasizes that

> the underclass is integrally a part of a larger economic process . . . that serves the living standard and the comfort of the more favored [part of the] community. Economic progress would be far more uncertain and certainly far less rapid without it. The economically fortunate . . . are heavily dependent on its presence.[7]

In other words, better-off people benefit from the lack of freedom of the poor. Our standard of living is enhanced by their inability to reject work that is unhealthy, demeaning, and inadequately compensated. It is in this sense that the poor are exploited. They are used in ways that rational people would not choose for themselves or those they care about. A comprehensive welfare state would increase the liberty of the poor, freeing them from the need to accept exploitative forms of work.

The third way in which the comprehensive welfare state promotes liberty is by equalizing the capacity of citizens to wield political influence. It would end the political domination that occurs when wealth can be used to amass political power.

I noted earlier that inequalities of wealth are acceptable under two conditions. They must not deprive people of the resources for a decent level of life, and they must not undermine political equality. If economic inequality leads to political domination, then the conditions for a just society have been violated.[8]

Recall that one of the key objections to state socialism is that it concentrates too much power in the hands of political officials. Capitalist societies (including forms of welfare capitalism) are subject to a parallel problem. Political power can become concentrated in the hands of the wealthy, who can use their resources to purchase political influence. They can do this by making campaign contributions, by using their own money to run for office themselves, or by funding the promotion of their own political views. People with fewer resources, even if they otherwise possess the means for a decent level of well-being, do not have these same political capacities. Their political liberty is limited by the disparity between their limited resources and the greater possessions of the wealthy. Unlike the wealthy, they cannot make substantial contributions to candidates, use personal funds to run for office, or promote their views by purchasing radio, television, or newspaper ads.

[6] J.K. Galbraith, *The Culture of Contentment* (Boston: Houghton Mifflin, 1992), 33.

[7] Ibid., 31.

[8] Walzer emphasizes the connections between injustice and domination in *Spheres of Justice*, xiii.

While I argued earlier that economic inequality is not inherently unjust, political inequalities of these sorts are inherently unjust. They are inconsistent with the central assumptions of democratic government. The idea underlying the slogan "one person, one vote" is that each person is to have equal power in determining the outcome of elections. When money can be used by some people to supplement votes, this undermines the possibility of equal political influence.

Hence, these forms of political inequality must be avoided in a just society. The political liberties of citizens must be equalized, and that requires both that current political "have-nots" be provided with increased political capacity and that current political "haves" have their political capacities diminished. Well-off people currently enjoy an unfair share of a valuable good that is supposed to be distributed equally.

There are a variety of ways in which political liberty could be equalized. One way is to limit the use of surplus resources for political purposes. Strict limits on political spending could be adopted. Alternatively, all election campaigns could be publicly funded. Or, people who are less well off could receive a political subsidy to help them pay for political activity. For example, people might receive an income supplement that would enable them to take time from work to run for office.

It may turn out, of course, that it is impossible to prevent people from using their greater economic resources to acquire undue political influence and power. If this is true, that would strengthen the case for an economic order that is more thoroughly egalitarian than the one I have defended.

I will not try to decide here whether the political use of money is something that can be prevented. My point is that such prevention is a central requirement of a just society. If the comprehensive welfare state is to promote political liberty, then it must go beyond providing people with the means for a decent level of well-being. It must take further steps to redistribute political liberty. As things stand now, political power is too highly concentrated in well-off people, thus violating the ideal of political equality that is central to democracy.

SUMMING UP

In this chapter, I have sketched an answer to the question: How much should a welfare state provide to its citizens? I have argued that an emergency relief model of the welfare state is not satisfactory, even though it is better than a pure market economy. As an alternative, I have described a comprehensive welfare state, and I have tried to show that a strong case can be made in favor of this comprehensive model.

While I believe that the comprehensive welfare state has many virtues, it will undoubtedly strike some people as undesirable. Others may think that it is desirable but impractical. Surely, there will be many objections to this model of the welfare state. Having seen some of the basic arguments in its favor, it is now time to see how well the comprehensive welfare state stands up to objections.

CHAPTER TEN

The Comprehensive Welfare State: Objections and Replies

I have defended the view that a comprehensive welfare state satisfies the requirements for a just society. Such a state guarantees all citizens the resources needed for living a decent life. By doing this, it accomplishes three major goals.

First, it maximizes well-being by providing all with sufficient funds to minimize the suffering and deprivation that are caused by lack of resources. At the same time, by permitting inequalities, it does not curtail economic incentives that motivate work and productivity. In addition, because it sets no ceiling on possessions, it allows better-off people to acquire luxuries so long as their doing so does not contribute to pushing others below the level of a decent life. Thus, it imposes no unnecessary deprivations on anyone, rich or poor.

Second, by ensuring the resources required for a decent life to all, it adequately responds to needs that people (humanly) deserve to have met. At the same time, by permitting inequalities, it allows for greater rewards in accord with personal desert. If some people can acquire more by making greater efforts or contributions, this is permissible, since they do not acquire it at the cost of depriving others of what they humanly deserve.

Third, the comprehensive welfare state provides people with enough resources to generate positive liberty, the ability to act in accord with their goals, intentions, and desires. By maintaining a private property, market system, it protects people from government coercion. Finally, it enhances people's liberty by protecting them from economic exploitation and political domination by the wealthy.

In spite of these significant virtues, many people oppose a comprehensive welfare state or have doubts about it. For this reason, I need to investigate the main objections that can be raised against such a state in order to see whether it can withstand criticism and whether it needs to be modified.

Some people may think that even discussing this proposal is a waste of time. The welfare state, they may say, is now widely believed to be defective and undesirable. Its flaws are so obvious that it is absurd even to consider such an extensive form of welfare state.

This view, while responsive to the political atmosphere of recent years, is misguided for a number of reasons. First, public opinion remains rather mixed and ambivalent about the activities of the welfare state. People who want to cut assistance to the poor so as to curtail illegitimate births, for example, often want assistance to continue so that children will not suffer. People who oppose big government and high taxes still want their own and other people's medical expenses covered. Many people want generous retirement benefits for the elderly and good educational opportunities for younger people. So, public attitudes are unsettled. Hostility to the welfare state is mixed with a desire for the goods it provides and sensitivity to the needs of people who suffer undeserved deprivations.

Opponents of the welfare state often base their opposition on the same values I began with, and I have tried to show that a serious commitment to these values should lead to acceptance of the welfare state and not its rejection. If I am right, then opponents of the welfare state must either admit that they do not care about these values, or they must revise their attitude toward the welfare state.

In saying this, I do not mean to deny that there are objections to the comprehensive welfare state that are worth considering. What I want to reject is a too casual and sweeping condemnation of the welfare state. This attitude, while common among some political leaders and citizens, is completely unjustified.

LIBERTARIANISM AND THE FUNCTIONS OF GOVERNMENT

One objection to the comprehensive welfare state is that it goes well beyond the legitimate functions of government. No one, it is said, should expect the government to provide the resources for a decent life, since providing resources is not what government is supposed to do in the first place. As the libertarian philosopher John Hospers puts it, "The only proper role of government . . . is that of the protector of the citizen against aggression by other individuals."[1] As we have seen, this libertarian view would oppose even the most minimal form of welfare state. Yet the view it expresses sounds plausible to many people and would certainly rule out the extensive distributive role that the comprehensive welfare state would play.

In considering this objection, it is worth noting that the libertarian view contains both a negative and a positive component. The negative part rejects

[1] Hospers, "What Libertarianism Is," in T. Mappes and J. Zembaty, eds., *Social Ethics*, 4th ed. (New York: McGraw-Hill, 1992), 335. Originally published in T. Machan, ed., *The Libertarian Alternative* (Chicago: Nelson-Hall, 1974).

all activities that go beyond police protection. The positive part defends the role of the state in providing protection against aggression by others. With this in mind, consider the reasons that Hospers gives to support his positive claim that providing protection against aggression is a legitimate role for government to play. He writes:

> If each individual had constantly to defend himself against possible aggressors, he would have to spend a considerable portion of his life in target practice, karate exercises, and other means of self-defense, and even so he would probably be helpless against groups of individuals who might try to kill, maim, or rob him. He would have little time for cultivating those qualities which are essential to civilized life. . . . The function of government is to take this responsibility off his shoulders. . . . When government is effective in doing this, it enables the citizen to go about his business unmolested and without constant fear for his life.[2]

I entirely agree with this argument. What Hosper does not see, however, is that the same arguments he gives to justify the government's role in providing all citizens with police protection are precisely the reasons why the government should provide all citizens with other resources that are necessary for a decent life.

Just as people cannot fully protect themselves against aggression by others, so we cannot fully protect ourselves against illness and injury, natural disasters, and economic and social changes that undermine our well-being. Naturally, we can (and should) take some steps to protect ourselves from such threats, but we can also take some steps to defend ourselves from physical attack. Yet our partial self-reliance in defending ourselves from physical attack does not mean that government should play no role in performing this function. Likewise, our partial ability to defend ourselves against natural and social ills does not mean that government should not assist us in doing so.

When government succeeds in providing citizens with the resources to live a decent life, then (to borrow Hospers's words), we can "go about our business . . . without constant fear." This is an important benefit of the welfare state. We can feel secure because we know that we will have the resources to combat many threats to our well-being. For surely we are not only threatened by other people's attacks. Many kinds of events and conditions can threaten our well-being. There is no reason why government should be limited to helping us combat only one kind of threat.

Like other libertarians, Hospers is particularly opposed to providing publicly funded assistance to impoverished people. Yet we surely know that people who work many hours at low-paying jobs have (to borrow Hospers's words again) "little time for cultivating those qualities which are essential to civilized life." Likewise, we know that the availability of work depends on many factors beyond the control of individuals. If our aim is to ensure that people have the opportunity to enjoy a civilized life, we must do much more than provide them with police protection. We must provide them with other resources as well.

[2] Hospers, *Social Ethics*, 355–56.

A crucial point that emerges here is that we need to ask Hospers and other foes of the welfare state not just to give their reasons why they oppose the welfare state but also their reasons why they favor a minimal state that provides police protection to people. When we do so, I believe we will see that the very same reasons that justify providing police protection to people also justify providing them with much more. The arguments that justify the positive functions of the minimal state also justify the more extensive functions of the welfare state.

The inconsistency of the libertarian view can also be seen in the arguments against taxation for welfare state purposes. Consider what Hospers says on this issue:

> Someone across the street is unemployed. Should you be taxed extra to pay his expenses? Not at all. You have not injured him, you are not responsible for the fact that he is unemployed. . . . You may voluntarily wish to help him out, . . . but since you initiated no aggressive act against him in any way, you should not be legally penalized [through taxation] for the fact of his unemployment.[3]

Hospers objects to unemployment insurance and other income benefits that welfare states often provide for people. He sees no reason why we should pay taxes to provide such benefits since we are not responsible for the misfortune of the person without a job.

Notice, however, that the very same argument can be given against taxation to pay for police protection. Why, I might ask, should I pay for police protection for the person who is being robbed or beaten across the street? I have not injured the crime victim. I am not responsible for his being beaten or robbed. So why should I be penalized through taxation and made to pay for the protection of others?

Again, it is clear that the libertarian is inconsistent. Just as the arguments for police protection also justify the role of the welfare state in distributing resources, so likewise, the arguments that are supposed to show that it is wrong to tax people to support welfare benefits would also show that it is wrong to tax people to support police protection. In fact, as I noted earlier, police protection itself is a welfare good, since it is a resource that is distributed to all, irrespective of their ability to pay for it.

The libertarian view of the functions of government is arbitrarily narrow. Libertarians are right that governments have an important role to play in providing people with protection from threats to their well-being. They are wrong to think that the only threats that government should deal with are threats of physical attack by other people. In principle, the comprehensive welfare state has the same kind of goal as the libertarian, minimal state. Both seek to protect our vital interests. Where the comprehensive welfare state differs is in recognizing a broader range of threats to our vital interests. This broader, more realistic view of the threats that people face leads it to a broader range of func-

[3] Ibid., 356.

tions. The rationale for these functions, however, is no different from that supported by Hospers and other opponents of the welfare state.

ENCOURAGING DEPENDENCY

A second objection to the comprehensive welfare state is that it encourages people to become more dependent on others and less able to care for themselves. If people receive resources from the state, so the objection goes, they will lose their self-reliance and other valuable traits of character. This objection, while often raised about programs to help the poor, can be generalized as an objection to a welfare state that provides resources to everyone.[4]

The worry about encouraging dependency arises from a certain ideal about the nature of the virtuous or good person. Good people have a certain strength of character that comes from taking care of their own needs and not asking others to prop them up. We admire people less when they rely too much on others and do not stand on their own two feet.

According to the objection, by providing people with the resources necessary for living a decent life, the comprehensive welfare state would undermine people's characters, making them less virtuous than they would be if they had to care for themselves. Indeed, one could argue that the amount of undermining is proportional to the extent of a welfare state's activities. The more extensive the state, the more it increases the dependency of its citizens.

This objection appears to play a large role in debates about the welfare state. Daniel Moynihan begins his book on the need for "welfare reform" with a first chapter entitled "The Problem of Dependency." He writes:

> The issue of welfare is the issue of dependency. It is different from poverty. . . . Being poor is often associated with considerable personal qualities; being dependent rarely so. This is not to say that dependent people are not brave, resourceful, admirable, but simply that their situation is never enviable, and rarely admired. It is an incomplete state in life: normal in the child, abnormal in the adult.[5]

Later, he adds,

> It cannot too often be stated that the issue of welfare is not what it costs those who provide it, but what it costs those who receive it.[6]

While Moynihan himself favored a guaranteed income for all (at the time he wrote these words), the point he expresses is often raised by opponents of

[4] In his influential book, *Losing Ground* (New York: Basic Books, 1984), Charles Murray claims to provide empirical evidence that the antipoverty programs of the 1960s and 70s harmed their recipients. For criticisms of his data and conclusions, see Christopher Jencks, *Rethinking Social Policy* (New York: Harper Collins, 1993), chap. 2; and Theodore Marmor, Jerry Mashaw, Philip Harvey, *America's Misunderstood Welfare State* (New York, Basic Books, 1990), 104–114.

[5] Daniel Moynihan, *The Politics of a Guaranteed Income: The Nixon Administration and the Family Assistance Plan*. (New York: Vintage Books, 1973), 17.

[6] Ibid., 18.

the welfare state. And he, too, thinks that it is important for people to work in order to support themselves.

This concern about the effect of institutions on people's characters is not foolish, but the specific worry about dependency becomes less clear when one thinks about it. The concern about dependency seems to rest on the following ideal: People should take care of themselves, and whatever diminishes their capacity to take care of themselves is undesirable.

There are a number of problems with this view. First, people who really want to promote self-reliance above all else ought to be anarchists. For, whatever role government plays will decrease the things people must do for themselves and will thereby increase their dependency. Even the minimal state that Nozick, Hospers, and other libertarians support has this effect. By providing citizens with police protection, the minimal state makes us dependent on others for our physical security. As Hospers noted, if police protection exists, we will be less likely to devote ourselves to target practice, karate, and the development of skills of self-defense. Police protection, then, increases a certain kind of dependency. Nonetheless, we do not ordinarily think that this results in diminished moral character. It is unclear, then, why dependence on the state for other resources must be seen as a lapse from virtue.

Indeed, when we reflect on this phenomenon, it becomes clear that the development of civilization depends on increasing people's dependency on one another. As Adam Smith emphasized, the division of labor is one of the central causes of increased productivity. It allows the development of specialized skills and makes for a more abundant product.[7] Moreover, it is only because artists, scientists, inventors, and writers do not have to take care of all their own needs that culture can develop at all. The price of both greater productivity and higher culture is a lessening of our individual capacity to take care of ourselves. People who think they are completely self-reliant are simply self-deceived.

Even the very wealthy are not self-sufficient. They rely on people they hire to cater to many of their needs. Often, they rely on money that they inherited from others to pay for these services. If they own stocks or bonds, they rely on many people in many enterprises who work to make their holdings profitable.

So, if the objection to the comprehensive welfare state is that it increases dependency on other people, then one is tempted to reply that dependency is an inescapable fact of civilized life. We are all dependent on others, and it is an illusion to think otherwise.

There is another point about dependency that is quite important. Being dependent on others is not always seen as a moral failure. Children and the elderly, for example, are not usually thought to be demeaned by being economically dependent on others. Likewise, the traditionalist conception of marriage, according to which men are "breadwinners" while women tend to the home and to children, involves an ideal that makes women economically dependent on their husbands but does not see the woman's role as less

[7] Smith, *The Wealth of Nations,* Bk. I, chap. 1.

valuable or significant. At least in theory, the woman who is housewife and mother is not thought to have less value as a person simply because she does not earn her own salary.[8]

In fact, of course, the traditional economic dependency of women often does result in a lower status, and advocates of economic opportunity for women have stressed this point. It receives some confirmation in a footnote remark by Moynihan. After discussing women who are dependent on welfare, he adds:

> If American society recognized home making and child rearing as productive work to be included in the national economic accounts . . . the receipt of welfare might not imply dependency. But we don't.[9]

This remark is interesting for two reasons. First, it draws attention to a widespread attitude that works to the disadvantage of women who work as housewives and mothers.

Second, it calls our attention to the fact that what counts as negative dependency depends on social attitudes. The difference between good and bad forms of dependency is, to some extent, in the eye of the beholder. We tend to regard people who do not have paying jobs and who receive a social subsidy as lacking in the virtue of self-reliance. On the other hand, we tend not to see anything morally defective in people who inherit an annual income. Yet both rely on others to satisfy their needs. Similarly, we tend to regard people who work for money as automatically displaying certain virtues, while those who lack paying jobs may be stigmatized for being lazy and unproductive, even if they work hard at raising children or do unpaid, volunteer work.[10]

In a comprehensive welfare state, everyone would be guaranteed the level of resources needed for a decent life. But there would be no stigma attached to this. It would be a benefit of citizenship, and receiving it would be no more demeaning than is the receiving of the right to vote in a democracy. (We can imagine a society that required people to earn the right to vote, and in such a society, the idea that people should get this right without effort would strike people as ludicrous.)

Finally, it is worth noting that if we are worried about people having valuable traits of character, we should recall that economic need can be quite undermining as well. It can produce forms of despair that undermine character. It can also turn people into lackeys and "yes men" who pander to employers who have the power to deprive them of access to the necessities of life. A market economy encourages its own kinds of negative dependencies.

[8] In practice, at least in a society like ours, not earning money may contribute to undermining women's status. My point is about a certain ideal rather than its actual working out in practice. For a good discussion of how economic dependence in marriage lessens the autonomy of women, see Susan Okin, *Justice, Gender, and the Family* (New York: Basic Books, 1989).

[9] Moynihan, *Politics of Guaranteed Income*, 17n.

[10] On this point see, Iris Marion Young, "Mothers, Citizenship, and Independence: A Critique of Pure Family Values," *Ethics* 105 (1995), 546 ff.

INCENTIVES, AGAIN

One of the most powerful objections to the comprehensive welfare state is that it neglects a key point discussed earlier: the importance of providing incentives to work. According to this objection, if a decent level of well-being is guaranteed to all, this will undermine people's motivation to work. People who work will gain less (because of taxes), and those who do not work will not suffer the deprivations of poverty. In the end, the economy will cease to produce sufficient resources, and all will be worse off. Because the comprehensive welfare state will destroy the level of productivity necessary to support its own activities, the proposal for such a state is self-defeating.

This objection has a good deal of plausibility and certainly needs to be taken seriously. But is it decisive? Would a guaranteed income undermine the motivation to work? While I cannot give a decisive refutation of this objection, I want to offer several reasons for doubting its force.

1. I cannot prove that overall well-being would *not* diminish in a state that guaranteed a decent minimum to all. However, neither can proponents of this objection prove that it would. Perhaps motivation would plummet without the carrots and sticks of unlimited economic rewards and punishments. Perhaps it would not. We do not know. The objection makes a prediction about the effects of a guaranteed level of well-being for all, but there is no hard evidence of its truth, and our tendency to believe it may depend on social dogmas that we have unreflectively absorbed.[11]

In fact, we all know that people are motivated to act by many things. Advocates of capitalism often speak as if the desire for monetary gain were the only thing that motivates people to work or be productive. Yet, all of us know that this is false. People have many sources of motivation. We want the esteem of our friends and loved ones, the satisfaction of doing what we think is valuable, the sociability that work can provide. We often want to be helpful and feel productive. We like to be challenged. So, there are many reasons why we expend effort. The desire for monetary gain is not the only source of motivation. We can see this from the fact that many wealthy people continue to work, even though they do not need the money. Likewise, many people offer volunteer services to various organizations, working hard without any monetary gain.

Even when people seem to be working for money alone, other incentives are often at work. People strive for economic success to ensure a better life for their families. That is not a selfish or a purely economic motivation. Even corporate executives or top athletes who seek higher and higher salaries do not, beyond a certain point, have any need or use for greater compensation. At a certain level, money takes on a purely symbolic value, functioning (like trophies or prizes) as a mark of esteem and accomplishment. Such symbolic rewards could continue to operate even if there were a guaranteed income.

[11] For a defense of the view that motivation is produced by socialization, see Joseph Carens, *Equality, Moral Incentives, and the Market* (Chicago: University of Chicago Press, 1981), chap. 3.

2. Even if the desire for money and goods is a necessary incentive for work, this provides no argument against a guaranteed minimum for all. While the comprehensive welfare state provides a minimum "floor" of income or goods for all, it does not impose any upper limit on what people may possess. Although taxes will take back some earnings and wealth, a comprehensive welfare state permits inequalities of wealth and thus leaves intact the incentive to work harder to make greater gains.

In this respect, the comprehensive welfare state differs from an egalitarian socialist system. While egalitarian socialists would forbid inequalities of wealth and income, a comprehensive welfare state need not take away the "carrot" of greater rewards. As I noted earlier, as long as all are at a decent level, the fact that some people have more is not an injustice. Because the comprehensive welfare state leaves intact the incentive to acquire more goods, it is not as vulnerable to this objection as an egalitarian socialist state.

3. It must be admitted, however, that the comprehensive welfare state does take a risk by removing the "stick" of economic deprivation. Will people work without this "stick"? Are there socially necessary forms of work that would simply not be done without the threat of severe economic deprivation?

This problem seems especially serious because some necessary forms of work are difficult, dangerous, and unpleasant. It may turn out that some types of necessary work are so bad that no one would do them without the threat of severe deprivation.

This may well be true, but it does not weaken my argument. In fact, recognizing this point is a two-edged sword. While it may seem to weaken my argument for a comprehensive welfare state, it also highlights the ways in which work itself can severely diminish people's well-being and suggests that one significant way to improve people's lives is to diminish the amount of terrible work they are forced to do.

If people were guaranteed an adequate minimum, they would not be forced into dangerous, dull, unpleasant work. Work would have to be reorganized to make it more attractive since we could no longer count on economic desperation to make people accept terrible jobs. Or, if certain kinds of work cannot be made more attractive, it would be necessary to attract people to these jobs by paying higher salaries for them. This would lead to fairer levels of compensation for many forms of work that are currently underpaid. Since a comprehensive welfare state permits higher levels of pay for some, it would have an easier time dealing with the problem of unpleasant work than an egalitarian socialist regime.

Other motivations could be drawn on as well. If work were more honored and contribution more socially esteemed, that might draw people to it. As things stand now, we tend to honor the wealthy and those in the public eye, while not paying enough respect to people who do many forms of valuable work. For example, we tend to honor physicians and to look down on people who collect garbage. Yet, the efficient collection of garbage raises levels of sanitation and thus makes an enormous contribution to people's health.

Without efficient collection of garbage, life in cities would be impossible. If we honored and appreciated people's contributions, rather than simply expressing conventional approvals and disapprovals of various occupations, this could increase the incentives to do valuable work.

4. Suppose that people who are able to work in productive ways simply cease doing so, taking advantage of the guaranteed resources to sink into sloth. And, suppose that this is a mass phenomenon rather than an isolated occurrence. As I stressed above, we do not know that this would happen. Nonetheless, if the prospect is sufficiently worrisome, there are a variety of a fallback positions to which advocates of the comprehensive welfare state can retreat. I will mention two less extensive forms of welfare state that can serve as fallback positions.

The first would be a state that provides a guaranteed minimum for all who are unable to work for pay. This would include the elderly, the disabled, and the very young. It should also include parents (or others) who are raising children since this is an extremely important, socially valuable form of work—even though people have not traditionally been compensated for it.

If we were to adopt this proposal, we would have a partially comprehensive welfare state that would substantially improve the lives of many people, while leaving intact the expectation that people who are able to earn a living on their own will do so.

A second alternative would be to set the minimum that is guaranteed to all at just below the level of a decent life, thus guaranteeing some amount of deprivation to act as a spur to work. Just how much deprivation would be needed would have to be determined experimentally. If our goal is to maximize well-being, however, we would want the amount of deprivation to be as small as possible. We would choose the smallest level of deprivation that would be sufficient to provide an incentive to work.

These two alternatives may seem to back away from my defense of the comprehensive welfare state. In fact, since they are fallback positions, that is precisely what they are meant to do. I offer them not as optimal positions but rather as positions to retreat to *if* the incentive argument is vindicated by experience.

Overall, then, the incentive argument may be less compelling than it seems. If it proves to be correct, however, there are alternative positions that advocates of the comprehensive welfare state can retreat to. Like the comprehensive welfare state, these alternatives would be superior to existing welfare states that fail to provide as extensive a range of resources to as broad a group of recipients.

DO NON-WORKERS DESERVE RESOURCES?

Another powerful objection to the comprehensive welfare state appeals to the following idea: If people are able to work but do not do so, then they do not deserve resources.

According to this objection, while it may be justified to provide a decent level of well-being for children, the elderly, and others unable to work, there is no justification for providing it to those who can work but don't. While everyone should be eligible for emergency relief, this is given to people only when they cannot provide for themselves. Normally, however, people should work to take care of themselves, and those who do not work have no justified claim on the resources for a decent life.

There is a further development of this objection. If some people work and others do not, then those who work will be subsidizing the idle life of those who do not work. This scarcely seems just. Indeed, it appears to be a new form of exploitation.

Note that this objection does not reject the idea of human desert. Instead, it says that people humanly deserve assistance only when they cannot take care of themselves. It denies that we humanly deserve more than this. If we can take care of ourselves, then we must personally earn the resources we need for a decent life. If we do not earn them, then we do not deserve to have them, and we certainly do not deserve to acquire them from people who do work.

This objection suggests a second problem that has not been sufficiently discussed by writers on economic justice. Most writers on this subject focus on the problem of determining what is a just distribution of benefits and rewards. Fewer consider the question of a just distribution of burdens. How can we fairly distribute the costs of producing economic and social goods? Surely that is as important an aspect of economic justice as the distribution of goods. I do not think, however, that it raises a special problem for the comprehensive welfare state, since every economic system faces this problem.

In any case, what can be said to the objection that people ought not to receive benefits if they themselves do not work and thus do not make some sort of social contribution?

1. My first reply to his objection is that people who voice it may not really believe that work and contribution are actually necessary in order to qualify for resources. In many instances, they permit and approve of people acquiring resources without making any effort or contribution.

Interestingly, the objection that people who do not work do not deserve a share of resources is echoed in a socialist slogan cited by Lenin: "He who does not work, shall not eat."[12] The fact that this slogan comes from Lenin should alert us to the fact that pro-capitalist foes of the comprehensive welfare state do not actually hold the view that everyone must work in order to have a legitimate claim to resources. Inheritors of wealth and those who can live on interest payments are generally not included when this work requirement is put forward. This is not a trivial matter, since a great deal of income comes from interest, and a great deal of wealth is held in the form of stocks and bonds.[13] As

[12] Lenin, *State and Revolution* (New York: International Publishers, 1932), 78.

[13] According to Edward Wolff, 20% of total household wealth consisted of stocks, bonds, and trusts in 1989. Moreover, for the top 1% of households, income from financial wealth increased by 66% between 1983 and 1989. At the same time, income from work increased only 23.66% for the bottom 80% of households. See *Top Heavy*, 20, 12.

a matter of fact, it is not a general moral requirement in our society that people must work in order to have a share of resources.

Nor should we ignore the fact that many of the hardest working people earn very little. Their low-paid labor subsidizes the lives of better-off people by keeping the cost of goods low. It was reflection on these sorts of facts that fueled the original socialist critiques of capitalism. Whatever errors there are in socialist theory, their claims about the unfair distribution of burdensome work and the failure to provide adequate compensation for this work continue to ring true today.

In making this point, I do not mean to suggest that everyone should be legally required to work. The history of forced labor programs is sufficiently horrible to make us wary of following that path. Indeed, recall that I am trying to argue against the idea that work should be a precondition for acquiring resources.

With this in mind, it may be possible to make a more positive use of the point that inheritors of wealth and holders of stocks and bonds are currently viewed as having a legitimate claim to their wealth, whether or not they earned it through their own labor. We tend to think of the guaranteed resources of the comprehensive welfare state as a kind of handout, something one gets for nothing. Suppose, however, that we thought about these resources as a kind of social inheritance or as the interest on people's share of the society's wealth. Suppose that every person received at birth a share of money, stock, or bonds that would be deposited in their name. This money would be held in trust and would become available at a certain age. If this were done, the recipients of these funds would be neither more nor less deserving of them than are the inheritors of private wealth.

Finally, suppose that instead of establishing such an individual account at birth, people simply collect an annual payment from the state, a payment that is sufficient to ensure a decent level of well-being. This is in fact just what the comprehensive welfare state would provide, and it would be no different from the social inheritance model. If we think that the inheritors of private wealth have a just claim to their resources, even if they do not work, then it is hard to see why the lack of work should discredit the claim of other people to their "social inheritance."

2. There is a second problem with the demand that only those who work should have access to the resources required for a decent life. This demand assumes that there will always be enough jobs for people and that our main problem is motivating people to do this work. It further assumes that social productivity depends on our ability to motivate people to work.

Some theorists, however, have predicted that in the future the supply of jobs will diminish so that many people will be unable to find work. While society's ability to produce goods will increase, its ability to produce jobs will decrease.[14] The availability of jobs, they argue, will decrease because technological advances will make human labor less and less necessary.

[14] On this issue, see Theobald, ed., *Guaranteed Income* (Garden City, N.Y.: Anchor Doubleday, 1966).

We can already see some evidence for this view. Many manufacturing jobs have disappeared as advanced methods of production have developed. Industrial work previously done by human beings is now done by robots. Likewise, in an increasingly competitive economy, many companies are downsizing, cutting the number of people they employ in order to diminish costs. If these trends continue (as seems likely), there will simply not be enough work available for people. If jobs for people do not exist, then the requirement that people work in order to obtain a decent level of well-being will be neither reasonable nor just.

The question that faces us is whether technological change is going to be a blessing or a curse for people. It could be a huge benefit for human beings, diminishing the need for labor and freeing people to engage in other worthwhile activities. On the other hand, if we do not make a social claim on these advances, then they will benefit a relatively small number of people, while condemning many others to lives of unemployment and deprivation. Which result occurs depends on how we understand these changes and what we decide to do about them.

The comprehensive welfare state fits well with the idea that everyone should share in the fruits of technological advance. Those who oppose this are, in effect, arguing that the benefits should flow to a select few. Yet, it is absurd to believe that a minority of people deserve to monopolize the benefits that flow from scientific, technological, and social developments that have been created by many people over long periods of history. Likewise, it is implausible to believe that people who are displaced by these processes and cannot find work deserve the deprivations that result from their inability to earn a living.

If those who predict a diminished need for human labor are correct, the moral demand that only those who work deserve access to resources will become unreasonable.

3. We need to return from this excursion into a future in which labor is unneeded, however. While the need for many kinds of work has disappeared and while this has jeopardized many people's well-being, there is still much work to be done in our world, and many people continue to work hard. In the present context, then, the generosity of the comprehensive welfare state may look inappropriate. A critic might assert that it is unfair that some people labor to support others who do not. Either people must provide for themselves (through work, private inheritance, or private investment), or they do not deserve access to the resources for a decent life.

There is some merit to this claim. Rather than trying to argue further against it, I want to see what follows if we accept it. Suppose we agree that (apart from those unable to work and those who do not need to work to provide for themselves) people should be expected to work as a way of gaining the resources for a decent life. If we insist on this, then justice requires that we accept two further conditions.

1. A guarantee that there are jobs for people.
2. A guarantee that those who work earn enough to sustain a decent level of well being.

If we do not guarantee both of these things, then we will be treating people unjustly. If we require work but do not guarantee its availability, then we are in effect denying people access to necessary resources. In addition, if we demand that people work but permit jobs that do not pay enough to sustain a decent life, then we are imposing burdens on people without ensuring that they derive the proper benefits from them.

If we accept the two conditions stated above (guaranteed jobs and adequate pay), we would be embracing another form of welfare state that is less extensive than the comprehensive state. Rather than providing everyone with the resources they need, this partially comprehensive state would provide resources only to those who cannot earn a living. In addition, however, it would guarantee that all those who are able to work (and are thus not qualified to receive resources) can find work, and it would make sure that their work pays them sufficiently well. It would recognize two important rights that are not recognized in our society: the right to work and the right to a decent wage for work. Neither of these is part of a pure market economy, so if they are to be recognized, they must be recognized and protected by the state.

I do not want to discuss how these conditions ought to be implemented. The guarantee that all work pay enough for a decent life could be achieved in a variety of ways—through minimum wage laws or tax credits, for example.[15] Which way is best can be determined on practical grounds. My key point is that the demand that people work is only fair if they get a decent return for their labor. That condition is not met for many people today. The so-called "working poor" work hard without adequate compensation and are thus denied the fruits of their labor. They bear the burdens of work without receiving a fair share of the benefits.

IS EQUAL OPPORTUNITY ENOUGH?

The final objection I want to consider appeals to the idea of equal opportunity. A person might grant that libertarians have too much faith in a market economy and might agree that the government has an important role to play in providing resources for people who cannot earn them by themselves. Nonetheless, such a person might object to the view that government should provide people with goods, insisting that the only legitimate role of government is to ensure that everyone has an equal opportunity to compete for goods.

According to this view, government should see to it that people are educated so they are in a position to compete effectively in the market. If they are given a fair chance to compete, that is all they can ask for. If they do not take the opportunity, then they have no one to blame but themselves, and

[15] See the discussion of this issue in D.W. Haslett, *Capitalism with Morality* (New York: Oxford University Press, 1995).

no one should supply them with an income. If they do take the opportunity but fail, then they cannot complain because they have had the same chance as others. That things have not worked out well for them is a misfortune for which no one (including themselves) is really to blame.

This is a popular view. Even a strong critic of the welfare state like Charles Murray seems willing to use the state to create opportunity. He expresses his approval of this idea and his rejection of going beyond it in the slogan "Billions for equal opportunity, not one cent for equal outcome".[16]

In spite of its superficial appeal, this "equal opportunity" view is inadequate. It fails for several reasons.[17]

First, Murray and other proponents of this view often contrast a government role in creating opportunity with a government role in determining outcomes. They want to distribute chances to earn an income but oppose the distribution of income or goods. Yet, opportunities are inseparable from outcomes. Children whose families lack an income cannot develop their physical and mental capacities in a way that will enable them to compete with more fortunate children. People without money cannot compete with people who have capital to invest. Even if the government were to provide a cash investment grant to all people at age 18, that would not raise the opportunities of poor or middle-class recipients of these grants to the same level as children of the wealthy. It would make opportunities less unequal, but it would not make them the same.

Ironically, while the equal opportunity ideal is contrasted with equal outcomes and while it is often invoked by conservative thinkers, the only way to come close to equalizing opportunities would be to have a genuine egalitarian society. As long as money can buy resources that are useful in competing, the unequal possession of money will result in unequal opportunities. People with more money will always have competitive advantages over equally able people with less money. Paradoxically, if we take seriously the ideal of equal opportunity, we will see that it requires equal outcomes. You can't have one without the other.

Even in an egalitarian society, people would not be equally able to compete. All of us have many different traits and features, and in different contexts, these features make us better able (or less able) to function than other people. Given the diversity of complex features and situations that create advantages and disadvantages, there is no way to equalize different people's chances to compete effectively. We can provide people with resources that are useful in competing, and I believe we should try to do this, for example, by improving schools in poor areas of the country.[18] Nonetheless, we cannot achieve full equality of opportunity.

[16] Murray, *Losing Ground,* 233.

[17] Recall that John Rawls also rejects this ideal in *A Theory of Justice*. For my summary of his arguments, see above, 90–91.

[18] On this issue, see Jonathan Kozol, *Savage Inequalities* (New York: Crown, 1991).

Moreover, as long as the conditions that make for success derive from circumstances beyond our control, the winners of the economic race will not fully deserve the rewards of their victory. Nor will the losers deserve their less desirable fate.

The ideal of full equality of opportunity is, I think, tied to a certain fantasy about competition and the deserving of rewards. The fantasy is this: If we could equalize everyone's chances to compete effectively, then the only difference between people's performance would derive from how hard they try. People who try the hardest would win, and given their greater effort, they would deserve to win.

This ideal is a fantasy, however, and it can never be realized. No matter what we do, different people will enter the starting line with different skills, attributes, and powers. They will not all have an equal chance to win, and the winner need not be the person who put forth the greatest effort.

The equal opportunity ideal, then, is not an adequate alternative to the comprehensive welfare state. People who advocate opportunity rather than outcomes do not see that opportunities depend on outcomes. Nor do they see that while it is at least possible to equalize outcomes (by distributing all resources equally), there is no way to equalize opportunity.

It is a mistake then to think that government should limit its concern to providing equal opportunity rather than giving people access to an adequate supply of resources. Where it is possible to provide these resources, that is what justice requires.

SUMMING UP

In this chapter, I have defended the comprehensive welfare state against several important objections. I have argued that these objections are generally less powerful than many people think. In a few cases, where a definitive rebuttal is not possible, I have suggested that a retreat from the comprehensive welfare state model might be necessary. Even these fallback positions, however, are much more extensive than currently accepted versions of the welfare state. This shows, unfortunately, how far existing institutions fall short when they are measured against the standard of a truly just society.

CHAPTER ELEVEN

The Bottom Line

At the start of this book, I suggested that concerns about economic justice arise naturally from reactions to three problems: the existence of vast disparities in the resources people possess, the lack of fit between what people earn and what we think they deserve, and the need for governments to establish a legitimate claim to the allegiance of citizens.

In concluding this inquiry, I want to return to these problems to see how well they are dealt with by the views I have defended. In addition, I will consider one final objection: the charge that the idea of a comprehensive welfare state is unrealistic and utopian.

VAST DISPARITIES

We live in a world of vast disparities in the resources people possess. While many people lack the resources for a decent life, others possess enough to afford many luxuries. How does the comprehensive welfare state respond to these disparities in the distribution of resources?

To raise the question in this form reminds us of a fact I have suppressed for most of my discussion. I have discussed the problem of economic justice as a problem within particular societies, but disparities in resources exist most dramatically between nations. How does the theory of the comprehensive welfare state address this issue? Is economic justice a matter of social justice—that is, a requirement within individual societies? Or is it a matter of global justice?

If there were a world government and all humanity were joined in a single society, then the comprehensive welfare state would take in all people. In fact, the world is divided into many different national societies, and this imposes both practical and theoretical limits on the demands of economic justice. Given these limits, my view is that for the foreseeable future, national societies have a primary duty to seek economic justice for their own citizens. This does not mean that they should be indifferent to others, but it does mean that the requirement to provide a decent level of well-being to all applies to members of particular societies. Emergency relief to others and assistance in supporting economic development are morally important, but societies have a special duty to achieve economic justice for their own members. Once their claims have been properly attended to, then more ambitious efforts on behalf of people in other countries become appropriate.[1]

Restricting our focus, then, to the distribution of resources within a particular society, how does the theory of the comprehensive welfare state deal with disparities?

Basically, the theory does not judge disparities to be inherently right or inherently wrong. Whether disparities are just unjust depends on the context. They are unjust if

1. Some live in luxury while others lack the means for a decent level of well-being.
2. Sufficient resources exist to provide a decent level of well-being for all.

They are not unjust if

1. All possess the resources for a decent level of well-being.
2. Those who possess more resources cannot use them to increase their own political power and influence.

There is a crucial difference between these two contexts. In the first case, disparities in resources are unjust because they contribute to deprivation, exploitation, or domination. This is not true in the second case. Because a decent level of well-being is guaranteed and political power is equalized, the disparities that exist do not expose people to deprivation, exploitation, or political domination. When disparities do not generate these evils, they are not unjust.

Economic egalitarians may argue that disparities in resources always generate the evils of deprivation, exploitation, and domination. For this reason, they view any disparities as unjust and favor ceilings or limits on resources in addition to a guaranteed floor. (Extreme egalitarians would insist on an equal distribution, while moderate egalitarians might permit some disparities, but they would limit them severely.)

[1] I discuss the legitimate priority to be given to one's own nation as well as the duties of nations to one another in *Patriotism, Morality, and Peace* (Lanham, Md.: Rowman & Littlefield, 1993). See, too, Michael Walzer, *Spheres of Justice*, (New York: Basic Books, 1983), chap. 2. For a more globalist perspective, see Kai Nielsen, *Liberty and Equality* (Totowa, N. J.: Rowman and Allanheld, 1985); James Sterba, *Contemporary Social and Political Philosophy*, (Belmont, Calif.: Wadsworth, 1996); and Peter Singer, *Practical Ethics* (Cambridge: Cambridge University Press, 1979), chap. 8.

If egalitarians are right that disparities always lead to deprivation, exploitation, and domination, then I would accept their view. They are certainly correct that these are the characteristic results of economic inequality in our world. Nonetheless, these evils are at least theoretically separable from economic inequality itself. Economic inequality is not inherently evil. Even in an ideal society, we may want to permit inequalities to serve as incentives or to reward those who make special contributions. We may also decide that enforcing limits on resources adds to governmental power in undesirable ways. So, we may have good reasons for permitting inequalities.

For all these reasons, then, the ideal underlying the comprehensive welfare state does not regard economic disparities as inherently or necessarily unjust. They are only unjust when they lead to deprivating exploitation, or domination.

THE PROBLEM OF JUST WAGES

What does the theory of the comprehensive welfare state have to say about what constitutes a just wage? How would it answer Tom Cottle's protest about the relative salaries of school teachers and baseball players?[2] Is that an injustice?

The view I have defended does not provide direct support for Cottle's criticism. Recall that his complaint is not that teachers cannot afford a decent life. Rather, it is that they deserve higher salaries by virtue of their efforts and contributions. Presumably, they would deserve more even if baseball players made less money, but the high salaries for baseball players (and others) seem to make the situation worse.

There are really three different issues here:

1. Do some people make too little money, even though they earn enough to sustain a decent level of well-being?
2. Do some people make too much money, even though others have enough for a decent level of well-being?
3. Is a system unjust if it permits people who do very important work to make less money than others whose work is less valuable (or at least no more valuable)?

Cottle appears to answer yes to each of these questions, but the theory of the comprehensive welfare state does not directly support his view, since it does not require income to be proportional to effort or contribution. Nor does it place any limit on people's earnings. Finally, by embracing a market system as the primary means of production and distribution, the theory does not impose a pattern of salaries that rewards people in accord with personal merit or desert.

Recall that a market system does not directly reward desert. In most cases, what people earn is not a function of what they personally deserve. Some-

[2] Tom Cottle, "Throwing a Curve at Our Teachers," *Boston Sunday Globe, Focus Section,* January 7, 1990.

times people's earnings increase or decrease as a result of hard work or high productivity, but this does not always happen. While the market permits this to occur, it does not guarantee this result. The comprehensive welfare state departs from a pure market system in guaranteeing that people receive what we all deserve as human beings, but it does not guarantee that people will receive what they personally deserve.

The situation of teachers may strike some of us as a moral injustice, but it does not strictly count as an economic injustice. While teachers' salaries may not correspond to what some of us think they morally deserve, it does not follow that the social system is economically unjust. The reason for this is that it is difficult to think of a practical way of institutionalizing our moral judgments about personal desert.[3] If we judge the market system to have certain virtues (high productivity, flexibility, etc.) and if these are incompatible with reward according to desert, then we will not insist that rewarding desert is necessary for economic justice.

Both market capitalism and the comprehensive welfare state, then, would reject the view that the wide disparity between teachers' salaries and baseball players' salaries is necessarily a form of economic injustice.

There is another way of understanding Cottle's argument, however, and here the theory gives him more support. Instead of interpreting his view as a claim about the unjust treatment of teachers, we can understand it as a protest about the inadequate resources being provided for education. Since education is an essential resource for people to live a decent life, inadequate resources for education will cause some people to be deprived of an essential good. Hence, the injustice is that those in need of education are not being adequately provided with it.[4]

One result of the inadequate funding of education is that there are too few teachers and those who do teach have too many students per class. Conscientious teachers will strive to make up for the lack of adequate resources and will be stretched to the limit in their efforts to provide a good education. They will be excessively burdened, forced (by their commitment to educating students) to work harder than it is reasonable to expect.

If schools were adequately funded and there were more teachers, then students would have access to the education that justice requires them to receive. In addition, if there were enough teachers, the burden of work for individual teachers would be less. Teachers would still do valuable work, but they would not be overworked, and they would not suffer the frustration of being unable to provide a good education for their students. In this situation, they might personally want higher salaries. They might also disapprove of high salaries for athletes. The force of their complaint would be much diminished, however, and the idea that an injustice is being done to them would be seriously undermined.

[3] For some of the difficulty of constructing merit schemes within professions, see Bok, *The Cost of Talent*.

[4] For a general discussion of this problem, see Kozol, *Savage Inequalities*.

If we reinterpret Cottle's argument then, seeing it not as a protest about teachers' salaries but rather as a criticism of underfunded education, then he is correct that a serious injustice is being done. The injustice, however, consists in the failure to provide students with a good education. If this were corrected, the salaries of baseball players would not matter.

This is not to deny that high salaries for some can have bad effects overall. In *The Cost of Talent*, Derek Bok argues that the extreme rise in compensation for some professionals discourages talented people from entering professions that carry out important work in society. Because pay for some business executives, physicians, and lawyers has gone up so much while pay for school teachers and government workers has declined, talented people are less likely to enter teaching and government work. The system of compensation as a whole, then, is socially harmful, and in the end, it results in a failure to provide important services to people.[5] To the extent that these lost services are essential for a decent life, the system of salary compensation contributes to injustice.

In summary, then, the theory of the comprehensive welfare state does not directly answer questions about what constitutes a just wage. Nor does it insist on compensation according to effort or contribution. Nonetheless, it can condemn systems of rewards when they result in a social failure to provide people with necessary resources (such as education), and this can happen when salaries in certain areas are too low or too high. Indirectly, then, discrepancies in salaries can be unjust, and Cottle's criticisms about teachers' salaries could be justified in this way.

JUSTICE AND POLITICAL LEGITIMACY

All governments place constraints on their citizen's actions, and all exercise coercion in implementing laws and policies. A continuing issue in political philosophy and in daily life is the problem of whether citizens have a duty to comply with governmental laws and policies. I believe that whether such a duty exists depends on whether the government and its policies are reasonably just. If they are, then there is generally a duty to obey laws. If they are not, then the law lacks moral force (although there still may be moral reasons to do what the law requires, such as refraining from murder and assault).[6]

Would citizens of a comprehensive welfare state have reasons for political allegiance to their government?

This may seem easy to answer from the point of view of those who benefit directly, receiving an income they might otherwise have been unable to earn. Surely it is in their interest to support this government. Note, however, that these people are still at the low end of the economic spectrum. Moreover, other political ideals (like Rawls's difference principle) might offer even

[5] Bok, *passim*.

[6] I discuss these issues in more detail in *Should We Consent to be Governed?* and *Patriotism, Morality and Peace*.

greater benefits. So, from the point of view of self-interest, the comprehensive welfare state might not be the best state imaginable for people who are less well off.

Still, it seems reasonable for them to support such a state and to feel that they are treated justly by it. After all, it provides them with what they humanly deserve. It does not ignore their claims to a decent level of well-being but instead provides the resources required for such a life. It takes the steps that are necessary to ensure that they do not lack essential resources, and it protects them from economic exploitation and political domination.

What about better-off citizens whose taxes are funding a guaranteed income for all? Aren't they the losers in such a scheme? Why should they support a comprehensive welfare state?

First, it is worth noting that everyone, even those who are well off, is a potential beneficiary of such a state. They themselves may fall on bad times. They may be set back by injury, ill health, natural disasters, or economic bad fortune. Or people whom they love and care about may be in need of resources of the state. Even if they never need resources of the comprehensive welfare state, all can benefit from the sense of security that such a state provides.[7]

Second, while well-off citizens may resent paying taxes and may believe that they deserve the full amount of their economic gains, this belief will not withstand examination. All successful people are in part the beneficiaries of good fortune. In addition, all people draw on the resources of their society, its institutions, and history to achieve whatever worthy goals they pursue. (In writing this book, I have benefited not only from people who have helped me directly but also from the countless people who have made libraries, universities, and computer technology possible, as well as those who have helped create the language, concepts, and intellectual heritage that enable me to generate and express my ideas.) The myth of the "self-made" man or woman is precisely that—a myth. Both realism and humility should lead all to see that claims to fully deserve all the rewards one possesses cannot be justified. Hence, fair systems of taxation do not deprive people of what they deserve. Because the aims of taxation in a comprehensive welfare state are legitimate and just, contributing one's fair share is a duty that one should not resent.

Finally, unlike more egalitarian ideals or Rawls's difference principle, the comprehensive welfare state does not forbid the well off from benefiting from good fortune. Rawls's difference principle permits only those benefits that raise the level of the least well off. In contrast, the comprehensive welfare state places no limits on benefits for the well off so long as others are provided with a decent level of well-being. Once others are at a decent level, there are no limits placed on improvements in the well-being of the well off.

[7] Robert Goodin stresses these points in *Motivating Political Morality* (Cambridge, Mass.: Blackwells, 1992).

There are, then, good reasons why a comprehensive welfare state merits the allegiance and support of both the best off and the least well-off people of a society. At least with respect to economic distribution, such a state would be a just state.

This is not to deny that such a state might be unjust in other respects. It might, for example, conduct aggressive wars against other nations or dispense benefits or burdens to its own citizens on the basis of race, sex, or religion. Its criminal justice system might fail to provide adequate procedures for trials or impose barbaric punishments. All of these practices and institutions would have to be considered in arriving at an overall assessment of the legitimacy of the state.

To say this is not to lessen the importance of economic justice. It is only to remind us that economic justice is but one part of justice. A government might live up to the standards of justice in one area while failing to do so in others.

UTOPIAN? UNREALISTIC?

Is the comprehensive welfare state defective because it is utopian and unrealistic? Is it impossible to create such a state? Would the economy of such a state survive? Would people work if they were guaranteed a decent level of well-being? Would taxes be so high as to overload the government and the economy? Could people actually be provided with the necessities for a decent life? Isn't this all just too good to be true?

One possible reply to these objections comes from Oscar Wilde, who wrote:

> It will, of course, be said that such a scheme as is set forth here is quite unpractical, and goes against human nature. This is perfectly true. It is unpractical, and it goes against human nature. This is why it is worth carrying out, and that is why one proposes it. For what is a practical scheme? A practical scheme is either a scheme that is already in existence, or a scheme that could be carried out under existing conditions. But it is exactly the existing conditions that one objects to; and any scheme that could accept these conditions is wrong and foolish.[8]

This reply grants the objection but denies its force. Indeed, Wilde relishes the charge of utopianism, claiming that only utopian schemes have real value.

Such a reply seems not to take the problems raised seriously enough. Practical problems matter, and they must be a concern to anyone concerned about achieving a just society. Nonetheless, there is something right in Wilde's response. If the problems of economic injustice are deep and systematic, any attempt to remedy them will necessarily look unrealistic, for what is being proposed is a departure from existing institutions and prac-

[8] Oscar Wilde, "The Soul of Man Under Socialism," in *De Profundis and Other Writings* (Harmondsworth, England: Penguin, 1973), 48.

tices. Our society does not guarantee an adequate income to all. Nor does it guarantee employment that will provide an adequate income. It tolerates severe deprivations, exploitation of people's misery, and the use of money to acquire political influence. Justice, then, does require large-scale changes, and the fact that it does so reflects badly on current institutions. As Wilde says, "it is exactly the existing conditions that one objects to; and any scheme that could accept these conditions is wrong and foolish."

Because our sense of what is realistic is dictated by what now exists, any proposal for serious change will always be unrealistic. Hence, those who propose radical change should not be too disturbed by charges of utopianism. Such charges are exactly what can be expected.

A second reply would deny that the comprehensive welfare state is utopian. After all, to say that it is utopian is to predict that it will not come about because it would require too great a change from our current ways of doing things. But if there is any prediction we can make about future events, it is that we cannot anticipate them. Events no one could have foreseen begin to look natural and even inevitable once they have occurred.

Some societies have taken steps toward guaranteeing a decent level of wellbeing for all. All developed societies provide at least some important resources to their citizens. As jobs become more scarce, as poverty persists amidst extraordinary plenty for some, the impetus toward greater justice may be strengthened and may emerge with renewed and surprising political force.[9]

We do not know what is possible, so we should strive to bring about what we believe is required by justice. Surely, we will hit obstacles and difficulties, but at least we ought to be striving for a just society. We ought not to let the difficulties become excuses for giving up or for rejecting this goal.

While the obstacles to achieving a just society are substantial, the ideal of justice itself will not go away. In part, this is because every society strives to convince its citizens that it is a just society. The ideal of a just society will live because societies cannot live without it.

Is it actually possible to provide everyone with the resources for a decent life? The answer may be unclear, but however difficult it may be to achieve this goal, actual societies will appear to be unjust so long as some citizens possess substantial resources while others lack what they need for a decent life. As long as deprivations, exploitation, and domination exist, societies will be open to the charge that they are unjust. This charge will continue to have force, even if the obstacles to improvement are real and difficult to overcome. The bottom line is that the demand for justice is unlikely to disappear until the requirements of justice are actually fulfilled.

[9] For the story of a reform proposal that was not predicted and that appears unimaginable in retrospect, see Daniel Moynihan, *The Politics of A Guaranteed Income: The Nixon Administration and the Family Assistance Plan* (New York: Vintage Books, 1973).

FOR FURTHER READING

GENERAL OVERVIEWS

Brown, Alan. *Modern Political Philosophy: Theories of the Just Society*. London: Penguin Books, 1986.

Cohen, Carl. *Four Systems*. New York: Random House, 1982.

Feinberg, Joel. "Social Justice." *In Social Philosophy*. Englewood Cliffs, N.J.: Prentice Hall, 1973.

Kymlicka, Will. *Contemporary Political Philosophy*. Oxford: Oxford University Press, 1990.

Pettit, Philip. *Judging Justice*. London: Routledge and Kegan Paul, 1980.

Sterba, James. *How to Make People Just*. Totowa, N.J.: Rowman and Littlefield, 1988.

ANTHOLOGIES

Arthur, John, and William Shaw, eds. *Justice and Economic Distribution*, 2nd ed. Englewood Cliffs, N.J.: Prentice Hall, 1991.

Combee, Jerry, and Edgar Norton, eds. *Economic Justice in Perspective*. Englewood Cliffs, N. J.: Prentice Hall, 1991.

Machan, Tibor, ed. *The Main Debate: Communism vs. Capitalism*. New York: Random House, 1987.

Sterba, James, ed. *Justice: Alternative Political Conceptions*, 2nd ed. Belmont, Calif.: Wadsworth, 1992.

CONTEMPORARY PHILOSOPHICAL WORKS: TEXTS, COMMENTARIES, AND CRITICISMS

Barber, Benjamin. *The Conquest of Politics*. Princeton, N.J.: Princeton University Press, 1988.

Blocker, H. Gene, and Elizabeth Smith, eds. *John Rawls's Theory of Social Justice*. Athens, Ohio: Ohio University Press, 1980.

Barry, Brian. *The Liberal Theory of Justice*. Oxford: Oxford University Press, 1973.

Daniels, Norman, ed. *Reading Rawls*. New York: Basic Books, 1975.

Kukathas, Chandran, and Philip Pettit. *Rawls: A Theory of Justice and Its Critics*. Stanford, Calif.: Stanford University Press, 1990.

Nagel, Thomas. "Equal Treatment and Compensatory Discrimination." *Philosophy and Public Affairs* 2 (1973).

———. *Equality and Partiality*. Oxford: Oxford University Press, 1991.

Nozick, Robert. *Anarchy, State, and Utopia*. New York: Basic Books, 1973.

Okin, Susan. *Justice, Gender and the Family*. New York: Basic Books, 1989.

Paul, Jeffrey, ed. *Reading Nozick*. Totowa: N.J.: Rowman and Littlefield, 1980.

Rawls, John. *A Theory of Justice*. Cambridge, Mass.: Harvard University Press, 1971.

______. *Political Liberalism*. New York: Columbia University Press, 1993.

Sandel, Michael. *Liberalism and the Limits of Justice*. Cambridge: Cambridge University Press, 1982.

Walzer, Michael. *Spheres of Justice*. New York: Basic Books, 1983.

Wolff, Robert Paul. *Understanding Rawls*. Princeton, N.J.: Princeton University Press, 1977.

CAPITALISM

Berger, Peter. *The Capitalist Revolution*. New York: Basic Books, 1986.

Friedman, Milton. *Capitalism and Freedom*. Chicago: University of Chicago Press, 1962.

Friedman, Robert. *The Machinery of Freedom*. New York: Harper & Row, 1973.

Hayek, F.A. *The Road to Serfdom*. Chicago: University of Chicago Press, 1944.

______. *The Mirage of Social Justice*, Volume 2 of *Law, Legislation, and Liberty*. London: Routledge and Kegan Paul, 1976.

Machan, Tibor, ed. *The Libertarian Alternative*. Chicago: Nelson- Hall, 1974.

______, ed. *The Libertarian Reader*. Totowa, N.J.: Rowman and Littlefield, 1982.

Narveson, Jan. *The Libertarian Ideal*. Philadelphia: Temple University Press, 1988.

Rand, Ayn. *Capitalism: The Unknown Ideal*. New York: New American Library, 1967.

Smith, Adam. *The Wealth of Nations*, 5th ed., abridged. New York: The Modern Library, 1985.

SOCIALISM

Bellamy, Edward. *Looking Backward*. New York: New American Library, 1960.

Bottomore, Tom. *The Socialist Economy: Theory and Practice*. New York: Guilford Press, 1990.

Bowles, Samuel, and Herbert Gintis. *Democracy and Capitalism*. New York: Basic Books, 1987.

Carens, Joseph. *Equality, Moral Incentives, and the Market*. Chicago: University of Chicago Press, 1981.

Crick, Bernard. *Socialism*. Minneapolis: University of Minnesota Press, 1987.

Fried, Albert, and Ronald Sanders, eds. *Socialist Thought: A Documentary History*. Garden City, N.Y.: Doubleday Anchor, 1964.

Harrington, Michael. *Socialism*. New York: Bantam Books, 1972.

Lenin, V. I. *State and Revolution*. New York: International Publishers, 1932.

Levine, Andrew. *Arguing for Socialism.*, rev. ed. London: Verso, 1988.

Lukes, Steven. *Marxism and Morality*. Oxford: Oxford University Press, 1987.

Mill, John Stuart. *On Socialism*. Buffalo, N.Y.: Prometheus Books, 1987.

Miller, David. *Market, State, and Community*. Oxford: Oxford University Press, 1989.

Nielsen, Kai. *Liberty and Equality*. Totowa, N.J.: Rowman and Allanheld, 1985.

Tucker, Robert, ed., *The Marx-Engels Reader*. New York: W.W. Norton, 1972.

THE WELFARE STATE

Barry, Norman. *Welfare*. Minneapolis: University of Minnesota Press, 1990.

Goodin, Robert. *Reasons for Welfare*. Princeton, N.J.: Princeton University Press, 1988.

Govier, Trudy. "The Right to Eat and the Duty to Work." *Philosophy of the Social Sciences* 5 (1975), 125–43.

Gutman, Amy, ed. *Democracy and the Welfare State.* Princeton, N.J.: Princeton University Press, 1988.

Haslett, D.W. *Capitalism With Morality.* New York: Oxford University Press, 1995.

Marmor, Theodore; Mashaw, Jerry; and Harvey, Philip. *America's Misunderstood Welfare State.* New York: Basic Books, 1990.

Murray, Charles. *Losing Ground.* New York: Basic Books, 1984.

National Conference of Catholic Bishops. *Economic Justice for All.* U. S. Catholic Conference, 1986.

Okun, Arthur. *Equality and Efficiency: The Great Tradeoff.* Washington, D.C.: Brookings Institution, 1975.

Pierson, Christopher. *Beyond the Welfare State?* University Park, Pa.: Pennsylvania State University Press, 1991.

RELATED ISSUES

Bok, Derek. *The Cost of Talent.* New York: The Free Press, 1993.

Dahl, Robert. *A Preface to Economic Democracy.* Berkeley: University of California Press, 1985.

Dyke, Charles. *Philosophy of Economics.* Englewood Cliffs, N.J.: Prentice Hall, 1981.

Fishkin, James. *Justice, Equal Opportunity, and the Family.* New Haven, Conn.: Yale University Press, 1983.

Goodin, Robert. *Motivating Political Morality.* Cambridge, Mass.: Blackwell, 1992.

Gordon, Scott. *Welfare, Justice, and Freedom.* New York: Columbia University Press, 1980.

Griffin, James. *Well-Being.* Oxford: Oxford University Press, 1986.

Lindblom, Charles. *Politics and Markets.* New York: Basic Books, 1977.

Miller, David, ed. *Liberty.* Oxford: Oxford University Press, 1991.

Rae, Douglas, with Yates, Douglas; Hochschild, Jennifer; Marone, Joseph; and Fessler, Carol. *Equalities.* Cambridge, Mass.: Harvard University Press, 1981.

Reiman, Jeffrey. *The Rich Get Richer and the Poor Get Prison,* 3rd ed. New York: Macmillan, 1990.

Shue, Henry. *Basic Rights.* Princeton, N.J.: Princeton University Press, 1980.

Index